# From a Child's Eyes

### The Paradox of Phnom Penh

John A. Stancik

# FROM A CHILD'S EYES
## THE PARADOX OF PHNOM PENH

iUniverse books may be ordered through booksellers or by contacting:

iUniverse
1663 Liberty Drive
Bloomington, IN 47403
www.iuniverse.com
1-800-Authors (1-800-288-4677)

ISBN: 978-1-4917-9292-6 (sc)
ISBN: 978-1-4917-9293-3 (hc)
ISBN: 978-1-4917-9294-0 (e)

Library of Congress Control Number: 2016904975

Print information available on the last page.

iUniverse rev. date: 05/18/2016

To my dearest Jan,
I wish I had been
with you sooner.
I missed so much.

Photo Editor for all sizing of photographs. Leslie B. Ocko, Ocko Graphics

Leslie B. Ocko
Linglestown, PA

# Contents

# INTRODUCTION
## Why do 24,000 homeless children live on the streets

This eyewitness report exposes the (deliberate) neglect of 24,000 homeless children living on the sidewalks of Phnom Penh that die for lack of food, and while city officials concerned with tourism, ignore the children's cry for help.

During the course of forty-three years working in the retail and cooking industries, I became involved in helping the starving and homeless in Scranton and Harrisburg, Pennsylvania, but did not have the time or resources to do more. After retiring in 2006, and a triple by-pass in Harrisburg, I moved to Galveston two years later. During my research of homeless children in other countries, I made plans to fly to Cambodia to fulfill the mission, and document the destitute children in Phnom Penh.

Spurred from an uncaring attitude by Phnom Penh's city leaders, and the facts uncovered, I was obligated to examine and photograph why society's rules allow these children to die. I also exposed why government places hardships on the homeless to live at the landfill, and the crippled and dirty children to roam the streets with no place to go.

Not waiting for the government to help the homeless in Cambodia, one advocate for the orphans, The Light House Organization, in Phnom Penh, developed a program to help as many children as they could ten years ago. Supported by individuals from other countries and financial aid from tourist, concerned Cambodians did what was necessary to aid these homeless children; symbolizing a positive approach, these volunteers are nurturing the young human will.

For further information, contact Mrs. Chea Savy, the director at the lighthouseorganizationlho@gmail.com. They are located at the Adoung Village Prak Pra Commune Khan Meanchay Phnom Penh, Cambodia.

The Killing Fields Monument is a striking memorial to the tens-of-thousands who were tortured and killed at the Killing Fields outside Phnom Penh.

The Sleng Genocide Museum where 30,000 men, women, and children were tortured and murdered within the city of Phnom Penh.

> I'm quite modest. I don't want to tell people I'm a leader
> Pol Pot (Died in 1998 at the age of 72)

> For in craving pleasure or in nursing pain
> There is only sorrow.
> Buddha.

Exposing how homeless children live in Phnom Penh it is essential to know why the working class struggled with their past, and yet, forgot those sleeping on the streets. After the city clawed its way from internal differences and external conflicts [The Vietnam War], the rift between the rich and poor grew larger. Even today, if there is any effort from the people demanding their rights, the military will enact severe and brutal punishment on the citizens who actively question the government.

Within the sizzling climate of a corrupt government, It is difficult for the poor to participate in the city's expansion, while holding on to their traditional values, yet they try. This culture's Buddhist teachings emphasizes caring for the young and elderly, adhere to strong family beliefs, and to be mindful for those living without hope. Regrettably, words are not enough to care for the homeless child and the dying infant without food.

More than 90% of the people in Phnom Penh are Buddhists

Tourists visiting the historic shrines and temples throughout this charming city contribute to the financial growth of Phnom Penh. Unfortunately, what they [tourist] do not see are children searching for food at the landfill, or eating garbage in a back alley, or wait for a miracle from a stranger.

Walking the many city memorials, one absorbs centuries of history formed from centuries of a protected Kingdom Rule, and how today, visitors from Vietnam, China, and Japan relate to their own history.

I ask myself, why doesn't the city do something about the homeless children at tourist sites? My answer would be to allocate funds from both the government, and foreign investments to help the homeless. Then, if the elders in Phnom Penh make a concerted effort, the capitol can allocate enough financial weight to begin the process.

Another immediate answer would require posting security guards at these tourist sites to deter the homeless. Would the tourist then believe it was unsafe to come to Phnom Penh if security were present throughout the city? The answer is yes. The solution, improve housing for the homeless allowing them to gather in government sponsored resting areas, and away from hotels and restaurants. The government could also create a part-time jobs program for teens and homeless elders to clean selective areas of the city.

That history we share is following us toward the future
The few children who were tortured, starved, and lived through the Cambodian War, matured with emasculated and broken bodies, and a bitter awareness of life. Their limited offspring carried that knowledge that today makes up the average population below twenty-four years of age.

In comparison to those in other countries, the average age of people in the United States is 37.2, Japan at 45.8, Vietnam at 28.7, China at 36.3 and in Hong Kong 44.5, and in Phnom Penh at 23.7.

The problem for the city's future is interestingly serious. How does the government's program for the city's future, along with the needs of the rich, while disregarding the poor? I am not referring to the ultra rich or the dirt poor, but the majority of Phnom Penh's citizens, the middle class.

(T)here exists within this class structure, an assertive boundary for those who have a livable amount of net income, and those who have barely enough to feed their family. To appreciate this impasse one has to acknowledge the vision that Phnom Penh has for its future growth, against the needs of ninety-percent of the population

To know when the capitol became part of the Asian community we should look at its history. Phnom Penh began on the banks of the Bassac, Tonle Sap, and Mekong Rivers, when the people struggled with an idea, as all young nations do a desire to be more than a village in the jungle.

During its birth, the city of Phnom Penh [Krong Chaktomok, city of four faces] set in motion its journey into the future with strong religious and family beliefs. Phnom Penh was founded early in the 14<sup>th</sup> century but in 1434 Angkor abandoned its claim, and then four-hundred years later became the capitol of Cambodia by the Khmer in 1867. From that time a history of conflict would ensure, with bloody takeovers, internal wars, and the separation of wealth.

The skyline of Phnom Penh, reveals crowded neighborhoods, high-rises, and the striking blend of two cultures, the progressive and the ancient.

# CHAPTER 1
## The Land and People of Cambodia, Treasure Chest of Asia

By the early 1920s, the city of Phnom Penh was called the Pearl of Asia, and for the following forty years, the city and its people enjoyed a rapid growth. This was due in part with the engineering of a railway system leading from the central railroad station, west to the Pochentong Phnom Penh International Airport, connecting the outskirts of the city to the center capitol.

Wat Phnom Monument to the city's historical past, surrounded by beautifully kept flowers, and walkways weave through a peaceful park. It is near the US Embassy, and the main post office to the front near the river area. Wat Phnom gave the city its name, Pali, City of Four Rivers.

Phnom Penh occupies 262 square miles and has over 64-thousand acres of roads leading from the city to remote rural areas. Fertile farming lands, constructed to feed a growing city's need for fresh fruit and vegetables were adequate for the time. Unfortunately, with the increase in population and tourism the demand for additional quantities placed an added burden on the farmer, who unprepared for the rapid development of the city, struggled to supply the growing populous. Not in a position to purchase better farming equipment, or acquire additional land, the farmer's answer was to have additional children.

To that end, the sons and daughters, as young as five and six, aided in the families increase production, but regrettably, it had a downside. In addition to the grandparents who live with their sons and daughters, the farmer had more mouths to feed. Grandparents could do little to work the crops because of their advanced years, so the children, forced to leave the family, looked for food or money on the city streets.

A decrease in rural output, the government is forced to import the cities needs from neighboring countries. Increasing levels of imported produce help to fill the food gap for the city, but sadly, the local farmer does not realize the profit from those imports.

Even though the individual farmer has production problems, the Phnom Penh's Ministry of Agriculture, Forestry and Fisheries (NAFF), reported in 2009 that the overall production of Cambodian vegetables increased by 14.6%, from 2007 to 2009. As encouraging as these production figures are, the small local farmer is still competing with Vietnam's vegetable imports of 70% of the total demand Cambodians need.

A view of the Delta from the glory and bitterness of an iconic hotel

This 100-room hotel and casino, Hotel Cambodiana, with today's room rates from $83.00 to $300.00 had a long and troubling history. The Golden Palace constructed in 1962 in the central part of the city, is 10-km from the Phnom Penh International Airport.

The present hotel, surrounded by beautiful parks and International Embassies, changed with the forcible occupation by the Khmer Rouge in 1973. Pol Pot stormed the city and used the hotel to house his troops, while destroying much of the city and killing the people. Restored after many years, the hotel began rebuilding from 1988, and then reopened in 1990.

The educated upper class isolate themselves from the illiterate poor

Not so surprising fact about the majority of families in Cambodia, are the parents in the rural areas who are less educated than those in the city are, with 3.5 children, while the city educated have 2.8. Many rural families lack an education above the seventh grade, perpetuating the illiteracy cycle among their children that hinders culture class growth.

Between the wealthy and the poor, a major difference spans more than education, availability of jobs, and the unwillingness of the poor to improve their circumstances. It is a damaging mindset within the Phnom Penh government that carries on the practice of economic and intelligent segregation of the poor. It is about the school system and friends with cash.

This corrupt educational system has a negative effect on the uneducated rural and poor city family, as cities fathers focus on the progressive inner city wealthy. The city families who can afford to pay for their child's future, aided by government assistance, concentrate on educating their children to obtain a profession that will financially help the family, and by spending more time in school, helps the city's future.

Not all of the less fortunate live in the rural farming areas, for there are many neighborhoods in Phnom Penh that house a populous well below the poverty level. The percentage of people in Phnom Penh below an acceptable income is over 36%, and if we apply that worth to the U.S. dollar, FIFTY percent of the people live below the poverty level in a city of two-million.

A majority of the farming parents does send their children to school, and while they receive a minimal education, their years to learn are limited as compared to the city poor. The city children may complete their education through the junior school years, but when they reach a mature age, the city child drops out of school to support the family's income.

Paying for an education, Phnom Penh's corrupt school system

A government report uncovered In December of 2008, of a teenage boy's teacher denying his days education. The teacher forced the student to stand for an hour at the door, until the class concluded their lessons. "The reason the teacher punished me was that I could not pay her bribe." The boy eventually graduated, and later related this was not an isolated case among the teachers in the school.

He later added, "it is unfair, but the children and teens have to pay for just about everything in school." He also told the reporter, "our class time, exams, even tests require payment." The practices that if you cannot pay for an education you are punished, and sadly, denied the lawful right so many students outside Cambodia take for granted.

In the rural areas, the impact on the poorer families' children that cannot pay for their education suffer the most. These children will ultimately quit school, and then degrade to a social level below the more affluent children from the city. After graduation [they] the wealthier children secure those jobs that pay more and

In defense of the teaching profession, the average teacher in Phnom Penh receives a monthly salary of $100.00 to $120.00, well below their need to purchase food, clothing, and pay for utilities. Clearly, the majority of these teachers' take-home salary is noticeably lower than factory/garment workers who have less of an education. So broaching the question of either taking bribes from a child in school, or having enough income for the teacher/mother to care for her own family, this practice is valid. Teachers entangled in the pay-for-education-practice, are forced to supplement their out-of-school-jobs, and spend unnecessary time away from the classroom to plan their classes.

Conversely, the city elite schools pay their teaching staff a higher salary and more if the teacher knows English, and has a higher level of educational skills. The practice for the more elite teaching staff in these schools is also present, but to a lesser degree.

This same [elite] teacher/parents pay seven-hundred Riel for their own child's education, and is a common practice they also struggle with each month. Between the school and their family, the cost continues to increase, adding to an average of over $60.00 every month for every child. The amount left to feed the family from their teaching income they supplement with part time jobs, offering steadier hours and a regular income; the Ministry of Education does little to curtail this practice.

It is the farmer and city poor family having to pay for an education that suffers the most. Twenty-five percent of parents who pay for their schooling were not aware that their child is (legally) entitled to a free education by the government, no matter their age or earning status.

As part of the school system's problem, Cambodia's most pressing issue is the corruption within the government's schools, and outside agencies controlled by the government. Fifteen-million people live in Cambodia that ranks 14th highest in corruption in the entire world, and 3rd in the Asian-Pacific region. Influence peddling has become a moneymaking enterprise with many of the Cambodian and Phnom Penh's officials who have "rich" friends in attendance.

French architect Louis Chauchon in 1937 designed the Central Market, and at that time, the largest market in Asia. It is one of three major shopping centers in the city, selling everything from clothes, cell phones, pickles, to silk shirts, fish, cut pork, and hundreds of other items; it is a frequented tourist attraction.

An American living in Phnom Penh, survives with his social security check

A few blocks from the Silver River Hotel, one can savor Phnom Penh's history, and see the influence on today's city and its citizens. The Royal Palace Park at the Tonle Sap River hosts an array of riverside bistros, hotels catering to tourist, and a mix of local and foreign foodies. They all come to see the Phnom Penh of today, and too, the city of yesterday, the mix of French and Khmer.

Travelers from China, Japan, Sweden, France, England, America, and Cambodia's neighbors from Vietnam blend into a spicy international stew; a classic gastronomy as each country brings to the city, germane cuisine, culture, financial support, and citizens from around the globe.

Phnom Penh is also host to a combination of city and rural residents that co-exist in 262 square miles at 2,009,264 million people as of 2008. Compare to Houston, Texas, an American city of 2,161,000 million people that occupies 627 square miles, one can see that profiling this Cambodian city from a first draft is easier said than done.

Living, working, and vacationing in Phnom Penh is a cultural experience I was glad to absorb as many other tourist do, but staying here for any length of time would be detrimental to my health (it was, Ed.) The level of infections found here takes years off any Westerners life, and for a man from forty to seventy in the United States, his life expectancy here would be drastically cut by ten-years. I think, I would like to stay for another month, but I can't, I shouldn't.

This is a diverse city of philosophy, understanding, and experiences requiring training to survive, yet the health factor is the larger concern. A vivid example is a man I met while walking in the park.

I introduce myself. "Good morning, you're an American, right? His skin, as seasoned leather makes me asks the question, because I'm not sure where he's from.

"Yes, I'm originally from New York City."

"You live in the Phnom Penh?" I ask.

"I moved here many years ago," he says, then looks at me, and asks, "another American?"

"Yes, I'm on vacation for ..."

He continues, "I fly back to America once a year."

"Why if you live here do you fly back to the states?" I think, maybe this guy lives with a friend, maybe a woman, and he needs the extra money.

He tells me, "to re-establish my social security benefits," he was a bit coy about it, "if I don't go to New York City, Washington will remove me from all Social Security benefits, its crap, but hell, that's life in the big city," he laughs.

"How long have you been doing this?"

"Next month will be seven years," he stops walking, "it's the price I pay for a cheap room and food."

"Would you mind me asking how old you are?"

"Fifty," he tells me with a grin, "I also enjoy the people here."

Even though he was fifty, he did not look healthy and an etched face proved that he made the wrong decision to leave the United States to live in Cambodia. I think, he's happy, yet he's paying the price.

Women, Buddhist Monks, and white rice

While eating breakfast in the hotel's patio, I'm watching an elderly woman setting up her vending cases outside her home on the other side of the street. In the sidewalk display cases, she selling chewing gum, candy bars, and cigarettes, and behind her, colorful plastic umbrellas and flip-flops hang from the ceiling. The refrigerator, at the rear, has a hand-made sigh that reads, "cold sodas and water."

Here too, another woman pushes a cart down this same street, calling for recyclable cardboard from the small mom and pop shops and hotels. She stops to talk with the woman vendor, and after greeting one another, they pass the time of day on how hot it is this morning. After a few minutes, a buyer stops to purchase a pack of cigarettes and the conversation ends.

Three houses down from the vendor, two Buddhist Monks stop with blessings for a young mother and an older woman praying outside their homes. After the blessings from Buddha, each woman gives the monks a bowl of cooked rice. Within a few minutes, this street becomes jammed with students on bicycles and motor bikes passing the monks, as the children go to one of the many schools in the neighborhood.

Character of a big city; a recipe for disorder

French architecture of Phnom Penh and the makeshift wood and sheet metal housing was not the blueprint designed for the capitol city of Cambodia, but over time, this strained togetherness fortified the (obvious) class structure.

This unwritten arrangement accepted by all parties in the beginning, has not been the best in recent years. The culture differences were satisfactory, even tolerated years ago, but not so today. If you stay on your side of the street, one group will tolerate the other.

There are times that the poor try to venture into the more affluent areas of the inner city, but city officials halt their advance, and remove them outside the city limits. This action is not reserved just for the slum residents, but also to those in the capitol who try to expand their pitifully living conditions. The reaction from the rich, not wanting to wait for the ousting, venture out of the city center to live away from dirty elbows. As for the poor, they know their station in life.

In the suburbs outside Phnom Penh there is a dramatic and different face for the rich, with segregated cities, mansions in gated communities, and manicured lawns and shrubs; one might think it is plastic. These satellite neighborhoods, developed for the children to play in clean parks, and fountains, are constructed for adult eye appeal. The selected mini-towns are built away from the smells of congested roads and the poor, to secure the comfort zone of its inhabitants.

Elite communities advertising groomed grounds, house corporate leaders, and present a stark contrast to the one-story family home blocks away; another planned ethnic action. Sure, the rich have access roads leading to the center city areas, where boutiques and fancy restaurants await their money, but these same roads also return to the refuge of homes surrounded by metal gates.

Phnom Penh is a city for and about tourism

This city of two-million people hastens toward the illumination of a new age with hope and energy, yet cannot shake the shadows left behind from its birth, and the Vietnam/Cambodian War.

Phnom Penh has a memorable tribal beginning of flowers and gaiety, a kingdom of rulers and obedient servants, and because of this history their legacy of troubled times grew. It is this changing climate of surging modern 30-story buildings, colliding with the sprawling slums surrounding them that push against the people's conception of city ownership; a noticeable opening between the rich and the poor.

Cambodia's capitol is about the life of the hundreds of restaurants, hotels, private schools, colleges, and suave women gambling in the casinos. The city is about the mother with four children searching for food on the streets, it is a shack built of discarded blankets, and a twelve-year old girl sleeping on a park bench, dirty and hungry. Phnom Penh is about the elderly woman sweeping the streets, and the luxury cars passing her. This deliberate separation of life styles is unlike any other city in Asia as it continues to confirm the capitol as a "kingdom" oriented society.

Exporting the rural farmer as a labor force to Vietnam

On the other side of a opulent life style, Cambodia's poor number over 4.8 million people with 90% living in the rural areas. Agriculture surrounding the city is the primary activity of the twelve percent of poor farmer toiling in these rural areas, relying on a constant growth of fruits and vegetables. When production is down, because of no rainfall or during the monsoon season, the farmer fails. Fortunately, for the rich this problem does not affect them, obtaining their fresh fruits and vegetables from neighboring countries.

Each year the country's rural households deal with food shortages, and due to their lack of production, they become part of the poorest class in Cambodia. Their average household expense of 30% goes toward rice, so to supplement their income they look for other means to support the family. What they find, due to a lack of skills and education is a job that pays little, and usually is temporary, extremely dangerous, and unhealthy. Regrettably, the government also uses them as an export labor force to work in other countries; in some cases, the farmer dies from the hazardous work and long hours.

Reshaping brick by brick, a tattered people and a devastated capitol

Phnom Penh's violent occupation by the Khmer Rouge left gaps in leadership, and during Pol Pot's occupation of the city, a majority of the teachers, doctors, and government officials were murdered. After, the survivors needed to construct a new system of rules, one of which was a new mini class structure, and by its concept a firm adherence to authority and power.

After the Cambodian War each person was on his own to stay alive, and then to fill an organizational void in command. It placed on every individual that survived a maximum effort to continue through those horrific days. The more aggressive person established this new chain of command, and even though a particular person's intellect might not have been superior to others, his/her ability and forceful attitude withstood opposition. This assertion of the individual was imperative and quite necessary for the time.

A new level of take-charge-person was in command to root themselves on the bones and dirt of the murdered professionals, assuming the role as the new Alpha male and female. After the Vietnamese Army came into Phnom Penh, they aided those who showed a tough management role, and influenced the tier levels of authority, especially in government and the military. The new society in these groups grew through those first months and years, and flourished.

It is not to say that those scraping for food in garbage piles at the city landfill, or the manager of a restaurant today, came to be in that position because of the Killing Fields from 1976. Yet, after trial-and-error, those with a higher education took charge away from the initial leadership, and then restored the class structure that still exists today. Those new leaders only took others with them who were likeminded.

Do not dwell in the past, do not dream of the future,
concentrate the mind on the present moment.

Buddha

Railroad slums leading to Gold Tower 42, and the Phnom Penh Tower in
the center of the city.

The charm of Phnom Penh is lost among this shantytown, a slum area the
government will not face in a responsible manner.

# CHAPTER 2
## The Financial Stability of Tourism and the Increasing Slums


There will always be poor people in the land. Therefore, I command you to be openhanded toward your brothers and toward the poor and needy in your land. Deuteronomy 15:11

One consequence from the increase tourist trade and a contributing factor to the thousands of children roaming the streets is tourism itself. This tourist friendly city generates an inviting vacation climate from 330 hotels and 530 restaurants, and encourages travelers to visit the city year round.

Visitors can dine alfresco in front of the restaurants, and that is when barefoot children walk between the tables, pleading and at times demanding money from the patrons. These children confront foreigners and quietly stand with open palms and sad eyes, waiting for money before moving to another table.

Still, not every child receives anything for their efforts, so parents have more than one of their children walking from one table to another. The mother stands a few steps away watching them, and then signals for them to move to another table when the customer looks away, or tells them to leave. Sometimes they [children] do not leave until the owner forcibly removes them. Because begging requires long hours on the streets, only a few thousand children can tolerate this dirty business, and of those who do, a few dollars is worth the wait.

Being rude is not hurtful to the children's feelings for they are aware this is part of not getting money. It only seems unkind to the patron, and that is why some tourist will give money, so as not to offend, or feel guilty.

During the first two-weeks in the city, I stayed at the Silver River Hotel, talking with the hotel manager, Mr. Sok Tima. We talked about places to go and areas to avoid in the city, and of the homeless children in front of his hotel.

This afternoon, Mr. Tima and I are drinking tea in the dining room after lunch, and I ask him. "Do you care if children wait outside your hotel asking the tourist for money?"

Mr. Tima says. "We don't mind so much when tourist give money to the children, but unfortunately it keeps them out of school."

I ask him. "How much can a homeless child make?"

He says. "The children know that foreigners will give them cash, so they wait, and because the American dollar is highly valued in the city," He pauses "tuk tuk drivers for a whole days work make $2.50 to $7.00, and sometimes the children make just as much."

"He continues as we walk to the front entrance. "A dollar is meager by American standards, yet that little girl outside my hotel is having a good day, it helps feed her family for a day."

I say good-bye and leave the hotel for another walk around the city. Looking back, I think, will he chase the girl away from his hotel? He did not.

I later found on the Internet that a loan officer makes $10.00 a day, and a server in a Chinese restaurant earns $17.00 to $19.00 a month.

Leave your lose change at home before visiting Phnom Penh

Cambodia does not accept any type of foreign coinage in any retail establishment, financial institutions, or by the people, and especially the street beggars in Phnom Penh. Because they do not want to handle the varied coins from around the world, the country only deals with paper currency.

However, the government does print values of their Riel paper notes equal to the American 25 cents, 50 cents, and the higher denominations of $50.00, $100.00, $500.00, and $1,000.00, the most commonly used. Notes of $2,000, $5,000, $10,000, $50,000, and $100,000 are also used, but not by everyday citizens who deal with the lower amounts up to $1,000.

Prior to leaving America, I was not aware not to bring any coins with me so consequently, I had a Zip-Lock bag full of nickels, dimes, and quarters that I could not use.

After you land in Phnom Penh, make the bank as one of your first stops to change US dollars only into Riel notes, and always have the lower denominations on hand for tipping and handouts.

There is always adventure walking the streets

This is the third hot and humid day away from the comfort of the hotel, yet I want to find the seedier side of the city. Before I left the hotel though, Mr. Tima advised me not to walk in unfamiliar areas so soon after my arrival, but I threw caution to the wind and ventured off the main road and into one such area.

During this walk, a couple of pre-teens are walking toward me, and the first realization I am in their habitat is the smell. I think, is it from them or the piles of rubbish on the sidewalk in front of me, or the excitement of the moment that is causing my facial discomfort? The children pass, yet the tangy taste and heavy odor remains in the nose and mouth for a few moments. I think, this is the sting of the city streets.

In view of the high-rise buildings, a shantytown flourishes

When the train station closed years ago, the city's worst poor established themselves and developed a thriving community, only two miles from the central hub of the city. Living on both sides of abandoned railroad tracks, two-hundred or more of the city's poorest thrive, and only two blocks from the Russian Blvd.

On either side of abandoned railroad tracks leading to the hub of the city, these people live a life in squalor and filth. In the background, another 36 story high-rise struts its stationary glass and concrete painted face, inviting tourist away from the tracks and unsightly poor.

Within this rail-side community, the majority of the older people do not wear shoes, while some younger people own scooters. I cannot say their perception of happiness is the same as the workers on the bamboo scaffold at the high-rise, but it is as real and comfortable as they can make it.

The citizens living here sustain themselves by selling basic items as water, vegetables, fruits [no meats], clothes, and building items to improve their huts. If there is a need for commercialism, the poor will find a way to promote it. One or two of the older poor own a wheeled cart that they pull through this area of the slums, collecting from their neighbors, recyclable cardboard and plastic containers that they sell for cash.

As more of the city's poor move into the limit amount of available space, city elders should make a concentrated effort to study the unhealthy problems of disease and crime. Unfortunately, the government encourages their migration away from the tourist areas, and into slums outside the city proper. It is easier for Phnom Penh officials to not deal with the poor's problems, because in the future when the government wants to move them, they are grouped together to relocate.

Many of these huts are exposed with limited sleeping and cooking areas, while the inside personal items hang at the rear. Outside a few huts, rain barrels collect water for more than one family to use. One or two of the more thriving residents own a motor bike that helps all when large quantities of rice or vegetables become available.

The people do not present a picturesque sight, yet they have a working plan to live together and help one another. For many who cannot live in another part of Phnom Penh, this slum area may be rough around the edges, but it is home. This area is a picture of people on a merry-go-round of boredom and ordeal, muted colors and activities, yet the children amuse themselves by chasing colorful plastic bags down the tracks.

With these many huts too close together for proper sanitation, I think, where are the bathrooms? A subject that will not warrant further research. What is obvious are grandfathers sitting on crates in front of their huts. Too old to work, these worn-faced men sip from bottles of warm water, and give advice to grandchildren gathered around them.

Looking down the tracks, I think, should I take the chance and walk the tracks toward the middle of the community? I feel uneasy on being alone with a camera, and wearing better clothes, so I decide against it. Nothing may happen, but just my presence might be a threat, at least a concern for these people. I decide to use the telephoto lens and stay where I am.

Earlier this morning I went to the train station, and talked to a guard. He informed me that within a year, the station will reopen and the trains will once more run from the city to the airport.

I then asked him. "What will the city do to the families living at the tracks?"

He said. "The government is studying the problem."

"There are hundreds of people, including children who have huts for a mile ..."

The guard cut me off and walked away. I thought, the city can't fix the roads from the airport, so how do they expect to reopen the train station. It is unlikely the government will have enough money to fix the highways, repair the tracks, plus remove the families. The railroad slums will be around for a few years.

Follow up. The train station was renovated in October 2010, but not opened until 2014, and is only used for transporting some goods and oil tank service. It is no longer available to the public, because there are no passenger trains. (Ed)

Even the poor have standards

The poorest area in this part of the city is located across the road from the railroad poor, separating the two sections. The track people have labeled these unfortunates, trash. The area is much older, and settled years before the railroad system failed. The housing constructed with elaborate wooden bridges five-feet above the ground, are literally built on stilts. These people are noticeably worse off, and with piles of garbage and trash outside their huts, injures are a common factor. The residents here are also filthy, infected with diseases, and live as peas in a dirty pod. dfsdsdfsd

On the way back to the hotel, two young boys and a girl, about nine come up and stand in front of me with smiles that would suit a kid at an amusement park. Their faces are dirty as are their shabby clothes, but they only want to have their picture taken as they are, I oblige. I show them the results, their smiles grow larger.

Walking on the other side of the street an elderly woman in her late sixties pushes a cart, neatly piled with folded cardboard boxes on top and tied to the sides. She stops at the corner of a busy intersection near the railroad tracks, waiting for the traffic to slow down before moving across. She is a tired old woman, but has all day to make her pilgrimage.

These scenes of the poor, the children with smiles and the old woman make up one side of the paradox of the city. The obvious other side are the tourist, those with money, and the government that separates themselves from the slums and street children.

At the heart of the city, a little girl cries for food

At the Silver River Hotel, and while on the Internet, I find other slums close by that peak my interest. The site describes that in Phnom Penh a minimum of twenty (20) slums exists in an area a mile from the center of the city, and where over 2,000 families live in 281 slum communities.

These disturbing facts further reinforce my contention that city officials treat the thousands of homeless and street children as they do, but not why they allow the slums to exist. The photos exhibit the despair of these people, and as one might expect, the hopelessness and lack of will to continue. I ask myself, if these poor are a bother to city officials, why not deal with the problem?"

Leaving the security of the hotel, and within fifteen minutes I'm in unfamiliar territory. On a back street, a barefoot five-year old girl with dried dirt around her eyes stops in front of me. She's crying, yet with a weaken voice asks for money. I don't want to touch her filthy hands and she smells of waste. It does not matter where the poor live in this world, or the language spoken, begging has a universal sign language. I hand over an American dollar

Further from the center of town, a few hundred poor live on boats attached to docks, on the Tonie Sap and Mekong Rivers. Firmly planted on the shores of the worst part of earth surrounding the city, families are confined to fishing, and diving in the muddy waters for recyclable items. These boat people seldom venture into the city or other poor sections of Phnom Penh, and when they do, it is to sell the bottles found on the river bottom, and then to buy food.

These families will not make contact with one area of the city. Not far from the main highway running through the city, is the worst congested slums, three blocks, named, Front du Bassac Apartments. The slums are unfinished three and five-story buildings, and with the balconies opened through the entire apartment, multiple families live in each apartment. In front, acres of rubbish and garbage accumulated over time have made this section unfit to live near, yet hundreds do. These unfortunates forced to live so close together, cry in despair a sorrowful moan for food and water, and for decency.

The rising river brings out the rats and rotting food

Slightly less than 70,000 square miles of the city's boundaries, thousands of families and individuals live on the main roads that enter the city. On the riverbank, Phnom Penh's largest hotel and casino, Naga World Hotel & Entertainment Complex, shadows one of these shantytowns.

During the monsoon season the riverside camps flood, and with the already deployable sanitary conditions, the rising water turns this section into an unfit collection of swimming rats, and garbage. The people walk knee-high in this filth, and sleep on top of steel sheeting or boxes inches above the water's surface. The human and canine waste floating on top of the water makes for the foulest of smells and sanitary conditions, coating the people's legs with a thick brownish paste they cannot wash off.

There are no soup kitchens or extra beds.

Tourism is not directly at fault for the slums, for they have been here long before the foreigners began to visit the city. Travelers from China, Japan, Europe, and America did not cause these poor to make the decision to live in areas unfit for most humans, so I affix no blame any group.

It is part of the city's responsibility to address this major slum problem, and to close the rift between government expenses directed toward the tourist industry and the lack of care for their own citizens. The tear must be closed by a financially sensible plan that would include supplementing soup kitchens and from a percentage of the tourist expense derived from restaurants and hotels. The monies required to clean up just three of these slum areas would be monumental, so addressing all such areas is impossible. Over a five-year period though, a noticeable percentage of financial investment could be viewed that Phnom Penh officials are concerned for the poor; but that thought would be a mistake. (Ed)

In the past, the government has made an effort to aid the homeless and those living in the slums. Unfortunately, their efforts were not directed toward the individual, but more to setting up alternate areas for habitation [replacement camps] outside city limits. The city elders evicted thousands from the slums, herding them on cattle trucks, and transported them outside the city to settle on even worse land.

The government promised individual lots, housing and the necessary items to build homes, but this was the carrot before the donkey. Lies of an improved resettlement by the Phnom Penh government didn't happen overnight or by chance, but by planners many months prior, making this action unforgiveable.

The acreage they told the colonist to settle turned out to be flat, with no water supply, sanitary structures, or housing. After the city did their job of relocating their human problem, the housing eyesore was destroyed. The land was then cleared and new construction became available for investors.

Broken promises are the heritage left to the Sambok Chab's 1,500 households, and for thousands of families throughout Phnom Penh, forcibly placed on trucks, and evicted. The families were denied the right of counsel, or at the very least a voice in this matter. The aftermath of the government's "move now policy" left the people in a worst housing position, with no upgrades in basic life-style than before the eviction. What the poor have today is a bag full of broken assurances, no hope, and disease.

The overall count of evicted persons from Phnom Penh stands at 150,000

These families, individuals, orphans, drug addicts, starving and homeless people live in the country's worst slums surrounding the capitol of Cambodia. They do not benefit from the basic services provided by the government, and traveling into Phnom Penh to avail themselves of the services is nearly impossible.

Reports have surfaced by the LICADHO (Cambodian Human Rights Organization) that Cambodia, and the British Oxfam revealed serious violations of the citizen's basic human rights from this eviction, and nationally 10 percent were wrongly mistreated in a similar manner.

Numerous factorial and verified accounts by the government against poor slum-reddened people are noted in reports published by eyewitness accounts and International organizations. They [LICADHO] suggest Phnom Penh's officials will do what is necessary to remove the poor away from the city and out of sight of the hotels, shrines, restaurants, and tourist.

Life on the Tonle Sap, Mekong, and the Bassac Rivers

The city of Phnom Penh sits where three rivers meet, and at the end of an island between two shores of the city, the river-poor live undisturbed. Only here do the poor on the island live in huts above the water line. They have a productive life, but at the wider middle section, ongoing construction eats away at their section of the land.

The myriad of boats; sightseeing crafts, four-star hotel, and speed boats use the murky waters to travel past Phnom Penh. The people living on the river and on the tip of the island use these same waters for fishing. It is a family affair as the father operates the motor at the stern, while directing the boys on where to dive from the stern or port sides. The children dive from the boat, submersing for minutes beneath the cloudy surface for cans or other metal objects. Unfortunately, the young boys come to the surface with an empty net.

After a heavy rain, the boat people live on their boats until the water recedes from the land. Then, after the river settles, the salvaging under water proves beneficial from the debris washed down from miles above the city, and stirred up from the bottom.

The most frequented used boats by the poor are the Phnom Penh River Boat, the Needle Canoe, Cambodian Plank-built Boat, or the Long Canoe Boat. As those living at the dumpsite, the boat children practice their craft with the same intensity as those rummaging through landfill garbage for a similar outcome, a stark contrast to comprehend though.

Tourist shop for silk and from vendors selling roasted spiders in a divided city

Cambodia's capitol boosts an easy-going merging of native Khmer and French influences, but with centuries of a prickly mix of the rich and poor, cohabitation is as an estranged couple. For centuries, and noticeably in the last ten years, breathing the same air does not alter their views on how they want to live or beside whom. Pattern from diverse levels of society, and a rigid financial class structure, everyone knows their place on the social ladder.

Phnom Penh in the south embraced the beautiful French carvings on bank fronts, colonial homes, government ministries, and foreign consulates - adopting the many iconic Khmer figures. In the residential northern and western sections, the homes are squeezed together as cookie cutouts, housing the majority of the people. The center section of the city is a mix of lavish homes, commercial and tourist venues.

Penh is noted for its open-air markets, narrow side streets, vendor stalls and mom and pop shops, all leading through neighbourhoods to the luxury hotels and four-diamond restaurants. Many street vendors sell from hemp baskets, roasted Tarantulas, crickets, ants, grubs, and termites, especially during the Cambodian New Year.

During the last ten years, the capitol felt a dramatic increase with new domestic and international business ventures. New restaurants and hotels directed to the ever-increasing tourist trade welcomed the Orient, Asia and America markets. Hotels offer rooms with a choice of prices and services, and a varied cost range for back-packers to corporate leaders.

In addition to food and lodgings, a very liberal investment law for foreign speculators became available for new construction throughout the city. While still maintaining the old world charm Phnom Penh has been noted for, the city thrives on these new capital investments, merging with the established old money, circulating both from bank to business.

In 2000, investors could start a banking institution for around four-million American dollars. Today with the heighten interest in the city's future, Asia banks are required to have a minimum of thirty-million US dollars. During the last twelve years, trustworthiness in Cambodian and Phnom Penh banks has been difficult for bank managers to obtain, due in part to the lack of trust and the stigma from the Vietnam/Cambodian War. People are leery to keep their money in banks, as ninety-five percent of the adult population and many businesses in Cambodia do not have bank accounts.

Do not park your Lexus in front of the Central Market

Walking Phnom Penh's streets, one may not appreciate, but will have to accept the constant sounds of a hundred motorbikes and scooters. This city divided by more than time and cultures, and split by concepts, alerts the adventurous explorer within. Vendors on the sidewalk crushing sugar cane stalks for juice in a bag or fresh coconut milk from carts are a treat to watch. These people and the woman sweeping the front of a government building are testament to the resiliency of the poor.

While stopping during lunch, I watch a gray-hair woman cooking a noonday meal on the street corner in a charcoal fireplace. The fragrance of frying vegetables and sizzling pork in blackened cooking pans brings the locals to sit and dine. Her younger daughter sets up card tables with hot sauce in the center and colorful chairs on four sides. There are no checkered tablecloths, only chopsticks, napkins, and a few spices in plastic cups. Friends talk and wait to eat a meal for less than two-dollars, and for an extra twenty-five cents, boiled rice.

I am invited to stop and eat.

"Sir," she says, "would like to have some pork?"

I must be polite, but decline. "No Miss, I don't eat pork, but it does smell good."

"Would you like to taste a piece?" She scoops a few pieces of pork out of the pan, and offers them for me to smell.

"Yes, they do smell good, but I have to go … thank you."

She and the people at the tables get a laugh at my hesitation to take a bit of the greasy meat.

I take a couple of pictures, smile, and continue my walk.

Not everything is depressing for this is a beautiful and thriving city, even though the stark contrast of the poor and the wealthy is prevalent everywhere. It is uncommon to see an air-conditioned Lexus passing scooters and motorbikes, but when they stop at a traffic signal, they do stand out, even at the Central Market.

The elite of Phnom Penh lavish themselves at the top tier of society with money and influence, obtaining all they want with the help from a corrupt government. On the other side of the financial capitol, the majority of the middle class are strapped to pay for their child's education, and basic living expenses.

The dirty and hungry homeless live in boxes

While tourism is highly visible, another increasing and obvious number on the streets are the homeless children. They make for an unacceptable impression for first time visitors and an educational shock seeing hundreds of children living in filth.

To tell the story of this Asian pearl, it is necessary to show the variations between the tourist and the shadows. The foreigners who travel thousands of miles by bus over Asia, through Vietnam, Laos, and Thailand, or fly in from major cities in Europe, expect a pleasant greeting after arriving. The soiled and hungry poor that live in boxes also confront the tourist, but their impression is longer lasting.

The poor weigh heavy on the scale of offensiveness, but it is not about the sweet odor from rotting cabbage leaves that greet the tourist. Dirty clothing and crushed sugarcane stalks deliberately piled in the gutter pull at the tourist perception of an inviting city, and at times blend with the body odor of a six-year old who just soiled herself.

As one couple from China passes a riverside restaurant, a young boy of five stops kicking the can, and roots through the pile of rotting food on the curb, but unfortunately, only found orange peels to eat. This depressing tale is real, but many homeless are at peace, kicking cans, or adding to the pile of trash. It may be unpleasant to most, yet on the streets of Phnom Penh it is commonplace, and I am becoming use to seeing it, but I do not think the Chinese couple see the big picture.

Tourism in Cambodia increased by 23% to 2,577,500

To put in perspective the impact visitors from other countries have on Phnom Penh's tourist program, we should realize their effect on the city's growth. Formed from the gap between the affluent and the impoverished, the government contributes to the increasing homeless and slums as they cater to the tourist. The tourists are not directly the cause, yet city officials still caters to foreign currency more than caring for its own homeless, and that is the major factor in this rift. Rather than using monies to improve the lives of their own homeless [they] the government agencies concentrate on selling the cities pleasures than confronting its failures. With this not so subtle action, Asian countries overlook the percentage of poor in the capitol while continuing their financial support to a corrupt government.

International tourism increased to Phnom Penh in 2011 by 492,700, a dramatic rise, and well above official predictions. It shows throughout the city as tourists spent the highly valued American dollar on locally produced silk and iconic images. Unfortunately, after their visit, the foreigner leaves with mental images of unwanted children and rotting food on the streets, something the city leaders did not want them to remember. Still, the governments advertising and promotional expense of $3.5 million US dollars in 2014 was half of the budget for the Ministry of Tourism. It is the growing number of (new) tourist from countries that the city offers $12.00 to $400.00 a night for a wide range of cliental, by investing these millions on advertising.

The homeless and poor continue to increase as well with an estimated thirty-five percent yearly of the total population in Cambodia. With the rural farmer accounting for ninety percent of all the poor in the country, the government files these figures just as reference points.

How inappropriate, with the increase tourist trade the city neglects the infrastructure to the farms to aid the rural poor, the inner city's homeless, and the slum areas. Only budgeting for the increase construction of new restaurants, hotels, and shopping areas, it is a reasonable response. However, the requirements for rural vegetables from the farmer to have adequate highways to and from the farmers, hinders any financial gain for them. The government's answer to that problem is to increase imports of these commodities from other Asian countries to fill any lapse of production for the city.

Bon-appétit to tourists from China and Japan

Aided the effort for new and returning tourist, the communication growth for the city comes from Phnom Penh's fourteen major banks, three newspapers, and three telecommunication networks, and within the city, over 330 hotels.

After arriving in the city, tourists can satisfy their tasting pleasures from over 530 restaurants that cater to cuisines from around the world. Nowhere in any other Asian country than Phnom Penh is this concentration of diverse food experience is felt. This ratio of people to places to dine is only surpassed in cities as New York City, London, Paris, and others with a greater population.

Tourism statistics are encouraging to the Cambodia and Phnom Penh government officials, but they do not tell the complete story. Because foreigners visiting Phnom Penh see the brutal sights of the homeless on the streets, the government makes every effort to beautify the main highways into embassy row, and hotels with gambling casinos.

Ten international and Asian airlines help support the cities diverse needs flying from China, with Japan second and the Europeans following a close third. Tourist who arrived in the Kingdom of Cambodia, thirty-three percent came by land while over thirteen percent came by air.

Cambodia is fortunate to have the financial support from abroad, yet it is still a poor country, with a GDP per capita in 1998 at $280.00. While city elders budget to increase the growing tourist trade, the income of the increasing middle class continues at a slower rate.

Lavish government buildings line the major boulvards leading into the center of Phnom Penh.

Child trafficking is a profitable business for many foreigners

While flying to Phnom Penh, I thought, would I see exotic images of colonial structures with Indochina and French architecture? Along with these thoughts, Buddhist temples with vibrant blue and gold statues standing guard, and thousands of motorbikes on the many highways, flood my thoughts. This is what most tourists see after arriving in Phnom Penh.

Beneath this pleasant exterior, the driving force in the city's life comes from that something in all societies that neither can be tamed or pushed aside, nor repainted - the people. The high-rise office buildings and bank towers, the numerous hotels, restaurants, and the dramatic increase in tourism adds to the funneling of capital left by tourist, but it is the citizens that aid in the city's growth.

The spirit of its citizens comes from the hospitality of the Khmer people, and is quite evident throughout the entire city of two-million. It is the philosophy of the populace of Phnom Penh, who daily awake to another day of repeating the sameness of the previous day. However, this picture of cooperativeness' is not the government's view of how the capitol should function.

> Have compassion for all beings, rich, and poor alike;
> each has their suffering. Some suffer too much, others
> too little.
>
> Buddha

Tourist and locals visiting the Central Market see a multitude of vendors selling everything from kids' socks and little girl's dresses, semi-precious stones, cell phones to fresh cut pork and chicken. On the outside perimeter are small shops with anything one may want in cheaper clothes or food to go, and around the four sides the curbs are crowded with stands selling an array of items as well.

The people of this country are a quiet people, and the friendliness they show to strangers is genuine. I had found while walking the streets that if I wanted to take a person's picture and they refused, I would show them one of the many I took of other people, and then they posed willingly for me. Showing the results and bowing and saying thank you - អរគុណ (aw kohn), I leave them smiling.

The national religion is Buddhism, practiced by 90% of the total population

It is refreshing to be with these people, unlike in America where the norm for a majority of people is to be wary or aloof of others, and in the last ten years, aggressive. Every society has its pockets of thugs and hoodlums, but in this city of two million, the crime rate is down for 2012. Figures released from the Cambodian government encompasses, assaults, human trafficking of men and women and also children, related drug crimes, and gangster activity. The Phnom Penh's crime rate dropped in the past six months of 2012, yet child trafficking continues on the rise, for it is this business that is the draw of those outsiders to Phnom Penh.

Cambodians are not a violent people, but unlike the United States, Cambodians culture comes from centuries of a practiced religion with deep-seated family upbringing, and a kindness taught from birth. Maybe worshiping of one basic religion keeps the country united, and staying at arm's length from worldly desires.

International food chains, a touch of home

This city's growth from the thousands of tourist contributes to its daily workings. Yet it is the ordinary citizen, the vendors, albeit on a smaller scale that adds to the daily circulation of those accumulative Riel and American dollars.

Hotels and restaurants greeting the foreigners from abroad is a priority for the government, and not the street side vendor. But the combination from the chef preparing his madrilène (cold soup), to the hat salesperson on the street corner, the street vendor selling gasoline in plastic bottles for thousands of motorbikes, helps to fortify the tourist industry.

To that end, the city offers much to the European, and Asian investors to share in the city's expansion. The adventurous local entrepreneur has done their fair share to make this city grow, yet foreign investments are paramount for Phnom Penh's future. Adding to Penh's development, local business men and world-wide food chains see the city's growth pattern as a good return on investments. This is quite evident when the traveler lands at the airport and sees recognizable food chains.

A walk from the Mekong River to the Central Market

Tourists from around the globe delight in the old world charm of Phnom Penh, purchasing Cambodian souvenirs, detailed paintings, and colorful watercolors of the countryside and Buddhist temples. Because they represent Cambodia's history, the locally handcrafted curios of religious deities and elephants are items sold more than any other.

Hundreds of artists' works are on display and sold in many of the shops nearest the Mekong River, street 240 (artist row), three-blocks from The Royal Palace. As I have found, bartering is expected as both the seller and buyer negotiate on a price for objects that can be purchased from other dealers at similar prices. Both Siem Reap and Phnom Penh present a varied range of shopping settings, offering the shopper fashionable women boutiques, men's silk shirts, time-honored food markets, plus goods from local artisans and Vietnam.

Phnom Penh's two traditional and distinctive markets: The Russian Market (Psah Toul Tom Poung), and The Central Market (Psah Thmel), in addition to a modern shopping center, offer an abundance of Cambodia's handcrafted carvings of Buddhist and Angkorian religious statues.

In all the market places many residents shop for the versatile (Krama: ក្រមា), the checkered scarf unique to the Khmer people. This garment, usually in a red or blue gingham pattern can be used as a scarf, worn around the head as a bandanna, or to carry infants as a hammock, and is the country's national symbol; worn by men and women alike. The Khmer Rouge used this exclusively as their identifying badge of honor and solidarity.

Phnom Penh's artisans boast hand-pounded copper and silverworks, colored gem jewelry, basketry, and Cambodia's national treasure, its famous hand-loomed silks. The silk made with patience and attention to the smallest detail and unique designs is valued worldwide.

The Cambodian silk industry, tailor made for Phnom Penh's Economy

One notable area for locally handmade silk items is a lake outside the city limits of Phnom Penh, and in the center, a large community of farmers and artisans have lived for thirty-years. Our tuk tuk driver, who also lives there, invited Berta and me to visit with him, his grandmother, wife, and their two daughters. They wanted us to spend a few hours in their home and watch them make colorful dyes, and the silk garments they create on a century-old loom.

I ask Berta. "You want to see the Russian Market today, or would you like to stay here and see how they make silk?"

"We can go to the market tomorrow, but to see hand-made silk, well," she paused, looked at me, and smiled, "yes, let's go with our driver."

Arriving at his home, we learned the art of making silk into women's shawls, bed covers and men's waist wraps. On a center display table hundreds of brilliant colored silk items of deep purple, brilliant greens, flaming orange and yellows, and vibrant reds captured our eyes. Their complex designs made into scarves, tablecloths, and bedspreads are the exact items they sell for double the price at the Russian and Central Markets.

The father, our driver, shows how he makes their own dyes from berries, leaves, and other native plants, thread the silk, and then loom the soft richly colored strands of silk into patterns of animals, temples, and mountains scenes. Before we leave, I purchase a beautiful shawl, say goodbye, and with the driver return to the mainland with a luxuriously colored red and orange woman's silk shawl.

A high-rise under construction near the Sihanouk Boulevard is one of many the city planners are building to invite foreign investors. The scaffold used is similar to how most of the building construction is completed.

Government troops and city police have the upper hand

On the reverse side of the cities glitter, there is a silent distress call from the families and children that are not part of the (colorful) environment of the tourist. The images are all too real for the homeless who have given up asking for help.

All too common to ignore are teenage boys roaming the park intimidating tourist for money, or a little boy selling small birds from dirty cages. These daily sights are widespread on the Wat Botum Vathey (Wat Bottom Park) across from the Royal Palace, blocks from street side bistros, and hotels.

Further, in the interior of the old section of the city, between streets 316 and 330, the poor have isolated this area for themselves. One such family, a mother, father, and three children live against the outside wall of a Buddhist Temple. The monks do not seem to mind this family, but eventually, someone in authority will tell the family to leave, and only then will they find another more peaceful area.

Thousands of street children and families are not the plague of the city, but their numbers are an epidemic nuisance to the tourist and the restaurant owners. They are dirty from not bathing, wear clothes I would consider rags, and their body odor is unsettling. They camp in abandoned construction pipes, garbage dumps, or land no one else wants to live in, and because of their growing numbers gravitate outward to tourist venues. The children are not contagious, and cannot help their appearance or their infected bodies, but only ask for something to eat and water to drink. Bathing is secondary.

City officials do little to help the deployable living conditions of the homeless, other than forcing upon them harsh evictions by the military into resettlement sections far removed from the city. Maybe the city leaders are correct not to be concerned, for the problem is too immense to consider fixing, other than the strict rule of replacement to land that is unfit for construction.

If (there) is a program in place then the system has already broken down, and any positive results to these "down-and-outs" is invisible. A dilemma too long overlooked, so why start now. "They will fend for themselves, as they always have, so another day can't make any difference." I thought, whoever posted that on the Internet, may be right.

Saying no to a begging child is not always easy

Pausing for a late Oriental lunch, a girl about six confronts me with her hand out. She's wearing a soiled flowered dress, worn flip-flop, and with dirty cheeks, one could feel sorry for her. She has been through here a few days ago, and now accompanied by her older brother of seven, stops at my table. Yesterday, I must have been marked as a soft touch.

> Work out your own salvation. Do not depend on others.
>
> Buddha

Trying to ignore them is difficult. I think, I don't have enough money or patience to deal with her and her brother. I continue eating, hoping the server will return and ask them to leave, she does, and the girl and her brother go to another table. I watch them leave and think, maybe tomorrow I'll find another place to eat, but the food here is delicious, so I'll return.

Restaurants and hotels promoting the beauty of their city are in conflict with the children, and the tourists eating alfresco. Still, many visitors give in to the annoyance of these kids, and give the local currency or the more valued American dollar so they will leave. For some tourist it is more than enough to force them to go elsewhere in the city to eat, while others feel sympathy for the children's efforts, continuing the cycle.

Cambodia is not as prosperous as the government says

A city of 2.3 million people, Phnom Penh updated their five-year program with special emphasis on re-establishing its place in the world community. Even though Phnom Penh is a popular tourist attraction in Indochina, and with the aid of international backers and local entrepreneurs, the city still has not regained its former standing.

While agriculture remains as the country's main source of revenue, Cambodia changed their economic plan in 1998, to an Open Market Economy, and since has seen a growth in textiles and tourism. While showing seven percent growth rate countrywide, other areas of production faltered. The per capita income is still lower than their adjoining countries, due in part to not cleaning its house of rampant government corruption.

Unfortunately, since 2000, Cambodia's government deflated their own shortfalls as their economy faltered from forecasted numbers. With unfavorable gains from a liberal work force, it became destabilized. Additionally, due to a soft business atmosphere, it also suffered from a decline in a firm fiscal policy with little positive direction.

Civil unrest of striking workers and a severe drought in 1998, foreign investments from Asia and China weaken the shipments of fruits, vegetables, and rice. Fortunately, in 1999, the government made internal policy adjustments, while passing economic reforms; the growth rate came back to four percent. The country enjoyed a noticeable period of peace after 30 years of internal conflict.

Major financial institutions from France, Japan, and Australia continue to support the economic growth in Cambodia and Phnom Penh in the last decade. Their approach is to provide aggressive capital to the government, because Cambodia assured the international investor a solid growth plan for the next five-years.

The spirited tuk tuk driver and the innocent tourist

The city has shown a notable increase in tourism over the last ten-years, unfortunately, while the city maintains and develops its main thoroughfares, inner city streets remain in need of repair with some sections of Phnom Penh abandoned. Lacking (regular) road maintenance, plus vendors, and numerous sidewalk shops that crowd these streets, improper road maintenance makes it difficult for motorize traffic, especially during the monsoon season.

For those foreigners streaming to Phnom Penh from countries around the globe, it is important that first impressions by airport employees and city workers demonstrate their natural kindness toward travelers from the moment they land. Later, as they shop at the many markets and boutiques around the city, the vendors continue the friendly welcome.

The reaction of the people's friendliness continues with the first ride in a tuk tuk from the airport to the city, as tourist become part of the brigade of hundreds of scooters and motorbikes traveling the Russian Boulevard.

Leaving the airport, tuk tuks will take the tourist through the city and direct to the hotel, because most drivers know the hotels or at least the streets in the city. Later, these drivers will offer an assortment of sightseeing package deals when you choose three or more sites for a nominal charge. Due to the competitiveness of tuk tuk drivers, many offer all day rates that include four to eight popular scenic stops, including the Vietnam/Cambodian Soldiers Monument and the Russian Market.

The rates are reasonable, but one can barter for a lower price especially for shorter city trips. The longer rides to the more distant sites, The Killing Fields, are firm. I found however, the drivers are fair because they know the city quite well, and seldom-over charge, and because the majority of tourist would rather ride than walk, the drivers offer reasonable rates.

The economy of Cambodia and Phnom Penh had their precarious and satisfying times, and during their re-emerging into the world community, Phnom Penh's decision altered the country and today's capitol as the shining star of Asia. Even with the corruption, the city continues on a set program of Economic Improvement, enticing Asian and Indochina countries to continue investing in their future.

Presently, I'm staying at the Silver River Hotel with a daily rate of $38.00, and that includes a free buffet breakfast, available laundry and Internet service, plus helpful hints and suggestions on where to visit. Wi-Fi, laundry services, and security, plus other customer-oriented features do differ with each hotel, but prior to leaving Texas, I found they are in a good location to the river and the rates to services was one of the beat.

Tourist cannot see the turmoil in Phnom Penh

In an effort to accommodate the influx of tourist from around the globe, the city still has the frustrating problem of staying ahead of the growing homeless on the sidewalks. City authorities realize they cannot repair a way of life for the thousands of needy, yet with hundreds of hotels, and restaurants, plus the many shopping areas, they hope the tourist will over-look the shabby five-year old girl begging at the entrance to their hotel.

Tourist cannot always see the underlining turmoil of the classes, or realize that four different security forces are on alert for peaceful demonstrators somewhere in the city, nevertheless, it [chaos] is there

# CHAPTER 3
## We the People do not have the Same Rights

Phnom Penh, capitol of Cambodia from 1432 to 1501 had many turbulent years, and as the country and the city went through a few historical events, the people stayed true to their traditions. Not all the chaotic years shaped the country, or did the peaceful times bring the rich and poor closer together, but all had a bearing on how its people became a society united by religious beliefs.

Divided by class structure, the dramatic result sprouted from internal fighting of kings and the common people, and through the years that divide grew. The country struggled to become a nation from a mix of violence and passive moments, yet ended up with the best importing and exporting poker hand in Asia.

France ruled Cambodia for 90 years until the country declared independence. After King Norodom Sihanouk's crusade in 1952, Cambodia then realized its dream of independence from the French occupation on November 9, 1953. Then, both the government and the people, while happy, had the difficult task to be self-reliant.

> If you give food to the poor, they call you a saint.
> If you ask why the poor have no food,
> they call you a Communist.
> Buddha

Today the country's foreign policy is about its borders, and from a lucrative contract established with their friends, Vietnam and Thailand, plus networking with China, and Japan, Cambodia's imports and exports flourished. In addition to the oriental market, the fiscal year of 2013, the United States exported $241 million dollars of goods to Cambodia, an increase of $15 million over 2012.

The nation's low wages, proximity to Asian's raw materials and an almost endless source of cheap labor aids the countries growth. Cambodia's dishonest teachers, corrupt politicians, and a constant struggle to rid the rural farmer from captivity of poverty, prove to be a yoke on the people's neck, and not the government.

Phnom Penh is open to both illegal and legal contracted imports, satisfying the daily buying needs of hundreds of thousands of citizens and the aggressive bargain hunter. Six major markets cater to their needs, carrying everything from knock-off designer watches to spicy pickles, and expensive liquors.

Additionally, there is this street-side system of individual and group enterprises that help keep the city collectively together. With multi-families selling their goods from the front of their homes, the local exchange of the American dollar picks up the slack at the bottom of the financial ladder.

What we think, we become.

Buddha

A typical scene as mobile vendors sells from bicycles, assorted baskets, mats, and woven toy boats. During the celebration of the Cambodian New Year, 2012 (The Year of The Dragon) many vendors flock to the parks to sell their hand-made goods.

South Korea leads the way as the major investor in Cambodia

In 2010 a trade agreement, of 180 million United State dollars, between China and Cambodia by the Ministry of Commerce of Cambodia, insured prosperity by the exchange of trade (imports and exports), and tourism.

During China's own economy expansion, the influx of the thousands of new and returning tourist from China to Phnom Penh continues to see major market growth. Due to this agreement, the economic effect secured the restaurant and hotel industries investments during the last few years.

The United Kingdom had been the largest investor in Cambodia for decades, but not surprisingly, South Korea poured into the country nearly $287 million USD, or over 12% of total investments. South Korea now leads the three major Asian investor countries, Korea, Japan, and China with a grand total of $762 million US dollars.

The future for Phnom Penh's children lies with breeding and culture

In tandem with this city's investment spurring new construction and further developing the tourist industry, Phnom Penh government officials have not forgotten about their biggest asset for the future, the [select] children.

Placing a strong emphasis on the education of the children in both the city, and in the rural areas, city officials encourage families to send their children to elementary school, and the more advanced child to attend college. The children of means, culture, and breeding are singled out more than the less educated as part of the government's plan for the future.

These [cultured] children concentrate more on the future for Phnom Penh, so they actively attend school to obtain an education in the business and financial fields. Unlike the rural family that does not see any benefit for their child's schooling any advanced education is unwarranted.

City officials are well aware, since the horrifying lost of teachers and professional business leaders during the Khmer Rouge regime, the overwhelming need for knowledgeable young professionals. They are conscious that the country lost the core intellect of this once great city in the arts and sciences, so they continue with the reconstruction of the capitol in all these fields. Phnom Penh's education of its children is sound, but the city and tourist still come first.

The Ministry of Education is a state controlled bureau that places the highest of priorities on all levels of educating the children. Intellectual development on a national level, Cambodia's Constitution states;

That the state shall protect and upgrade citizen's opportunity to earn at all levels, guaranteeing that all citizens have equal opportunity to earn a living.
Quote taken from Wikipedia, The Free Encyclopedia.

From 1918, the Royal University of Fine Arts (Khmer) began a teaching forum for the young creative minds of Phnom Penh. The Khmer Rouge in 1975 closed the school, but today the Royal University of Fine Arts has approximately 800 students, learning from five major facilities within city limits to continue the government's idea on education.

The main campus of the (RUFA) teaching Fine Arts, Choreographic, Music, Urbanism, and Archaeology is located on Street 184, Preah Theamak Lethet Ouk and is dedicated to educating a young generation to preserve traditional Khmer culture.

Phnom Penh realizes the educational system is vital to the city and the state. One main blockage for most students is that the majority of the schools are private, and so the average child does not receive the education all should receive.

Private schools in the city impress on the students to learn the English language, because it is the English-speaking tourist they will talk with. These private institutions hire English speaking Americans or those teachers fluent in the English language, more than Cambodian teachers. Harsh as it is, this thinking contributes to the gap between the privately taught student and the Cambodian poor who only speak Khmer.

This separation originates from a lack of formal schooling in a majority of the children of Phnom Penh's rural farming sections. With an estimated 616,000 children, ages five to seventeen years, they turn to manual labor other than schooling; working an average of five hours a day for low-paying jobs.

Unfortunately, over 33% of newborn children die a month after birth

Without a clear national program to regulate births, the rural poor are responsible for the larger family; more children are able to work in the fields. Consequently, government officials still ignore the national outcry to regulate and control this rising birth rate. This unregulated action limits the number of students from the farming country for a proper education, thus focusing on the middle-class and wealthy students.

The increased population has with it the continuing risk for childbirth deaths, even before the age of five; children die of malnutrition and common childhood disease that are more widespread in the farming areas of Phnom Penh.

The Cambodia Demographic and Health Survey (CDHS) in 2000 released their figures pertaining to a dangerous component of hand, foot, and mouth disease, as EV-71 that claimed the lives of many young children. Ninety-five of every 1,000 babies born in Cambodia die before the age of one-year, making Cambodia the highest rate of infants dying in Southeast Asia.

In a kingdom country, twenty thousand Christians are the minority

Despite the French colonization of Cambodia, their influence on the religious beliefs of the Khmer population did not sway those [Cambodians] toward adopting the Roman Catholic Religion.

Ninety percent of the inhabitants of Phnom Penh are Cambodians (Khmers), with Buddhism accounting for 90% to 95% of the total inhabitants in all Cambodia. Also, representative is a large minority of Vietnamese, and Chinese.

The population of Phnom Penh, in 2008 was 2,009,264, a growth rate of 3.92%. With international visitors, accounting for 3.58 million visiting the city in 2012, social services, and the hospitality industries become strained. Executives staying long-term interject personal and corporate finances into the city's economy, yet the system to support the additional numbers struggles.

The Khmer Rouge tortured and murdered millions

Cambodia, like no other country since 1970 through 1980, for its size and population, was unmatched in its suffering. By conservative estimates, guerrilla and government groups murdered millions of adults, babies, and children. During the Vietnam/ Cambodia War and with the ultimate takeover by the Communist Party of Kampuchea (CPK), known later as the Khmer Rouge, they suffered the greatest in the capitol of Phnom Penh.

The unparallel genocide of the 7,000,000 people beginning in 1970 resulted in approximately 4,000,000 people dying from that war, plus 35,000 foreigners. Foreign invaders, a brutal famine that lasted for years, murder, and the massacre of personal ideology significantly contributed to the overall deaths.

The CPK in Phnom Penh had the distinction of being the most fanatical of all Communist factions in Asia. They even turned on their own leaders and other members of the CPK, later believing they too were a threat.

The country (specifically Phnom Penh) became the headquarters of immense and sustainable massacres. Pol Pot destroyed the population at will, murdering thousands of Buddhist Monks, destroying all the Cambodian currency, and raising over 80% of the buildings in the capitol.

The Khmer Rouge slaughtered the male population

As with any aftermath of war, in 1981 Phnom Penh's problems of reconstruction and birthing of the populous became paramount to secure a blueprint for the new capitol. The survivors plan required immediate attention, with repopulation at the top of the list. A limited work force left after the purge faced a ruined city with little resources to rebuild.

> I never see what has been done;
> I only see what remains to be done.
>
> Buddha

After, the topic of marriage became a vital concern for the women who survived Pol Pot's purge. Months after the Vietnamese Army liberated Phnom Penh, hundreds of women realized the degree of the genocide of their country, of their children, and especially of the male population.

The mothering instinct was to nurture the children who were left, and to begin new families, but the limited number of males presented a hardship. Who was to rebuild the city? Who would father their children? Those answers came slowly, but the Cambodian women were patient.

> Health is the greatest gift,
> contentment the greatest wealth,
> faithfulness, the best relationship.
>
> Buddha

Decades later, women knew a good marriage was essential for both the bride and groom to rebuild the country. That both mates can provide for each other and for the children's safe and secure future, family members performed background checks on the mates, and on other family members to insure compatibility.

Today's courtship is quite different in the rural and urban areas of Phnom Penh. Westernization has influenced the openness in the city with an Asian-Euro attitude among the less traditional, with an open longer courtship. A romantic relationship with the closeness of partners expressing their love openly in public is acceptable and encouraged for proper behavior and long-term commitments.

Buddhist teachings say little on polygamy and monogamy, only that the male limit himself to one wife. There are no rules taught by Buddha on how to have a joyful life together, but that the man is faithful to his own spouse, and not have sensual thoughts for another woman.

Divorce in Cambodia is a horrible and offensive point to have hanging over both the man and woman if they would split, and in a country where religion is revered, divorce places a negative and scornful cloud around both partners. However, remarks by men admit that ONE in FIVE commits rape, and believe it is permissible.

In the country, the less educated adult maintains a strict tradition in approaching marriage, not as open but just as sincere as their city counterparts approach. In the rural areas, the man and woman are more practical and marry out of a need to father children to work. While both partners from the city marry between nineteen and twenty-five, as an average, the women marry from sixteen to twenty-two in the rural areas.

Regrettably, marriages in the countryside are likely to wed with blood relatives, and close neighbors a carry-over from earlier times. A traditional habit practiced by those outside the city proper is frown on by the progressive, educated city families, and the government. Country [rural/farmer] people continue this closed community marriage practice, because the law permits it, so the husband can financially provide for the family and take responsibility for the children's education before he dies.

With the openness in the city, the man and woman meet a broader range of people in their line of work, and socializing with people from neighboring countries, the need to marry early and with relatives is not the usual practice.

Cambodian law says that the woman must be 18 years of age and the man 20, and neither may be related by blood, and still with both these stipulations, it is not always followed, especially when a percentage of woman marry before eighteen.

Cambodian men live to around fifty-eight years of age, but not much older, so they tend to marry younger. Because the man has a higher death rate (more prone to diseases), teenage girls make their choices earlier in life.

I ask a woman how old she is, she tells me, twenty-seven

Personal observations from the walks reveal a population with an average age in the mid twenties. Even though there are elderly citizens working and retired, I thought, their numbers are less than I imagined, especially for a city of two-million people.

At a riverside restaurant during a meal of rice and vegetables, I begin a conversation with a charming female server. She is around five-feet, with deep brown hair to her waist, and brown eyes, and a refined maturity befitting the women of Phnom Penh. I guess her age at twenty or twenty-three, but after a few minutes, I ask. "Excuse me, but you look in your early twenties."

She says, "I'm twenty-seven. My husband left me with our seven-year-old son two-years ago," she pauses, questioning my intent, but continues, "and now we live with my mother."

I ask her. "How long have you worked at this restaurant?"

She tells me. "Two years, but I had another job cleaning for three years. I didn't like the work, because here I meet people."

"Is your son in school?"

"Yes, and is doing very well with his education."

Knowing about the pay to learn from teachers, I ask her. "Do you pay for your boy's education, like books and paper?"

"No," she tells me with a smile, "the government pays for all his schooling, and I'm grateful for that."

She supports her son and mother with this one job that pays little, and struggles to make every dollar count, and with no government support other than schooling, she still has a positive attitude. I finish the meal, leave a tip, and say my goodbye and then leave, carrying with me an admiration for one woman of class.

Allow Phnom Penh to introduce you to Pol Pot

Pol Pot had many slogans during his stay in Phnom Penh, but the one he was best noted for, talking about the Cambodians sent to the Killing Fields;

> To spare you is no profit; to destroy you is no loss.
>
> Pol Pot

The young professionals in 1970 and the people in general wanted to continue with their lives prior to the Vietnam War. Unfortunately, Pol Pot had quite a different and radical approach when his army invaded the city. He knew in 1975 what teachings were best for them.

Philosophy of the individual and the Khmer Rouge's posture on Communism were at odds after the take-over by Pol Pot. If you were a teacher or a professor you were a traitor to the revolution, and in the first few days, your life span was limited on how long you were able to endure torture.

Children and former students of all ages became recruits and were brainwashed to identify former teachers, and business professionals. The children became participants [tools of Pol Pot] in the worse crimes during the Khmer Rouge reign. The traditional way to educate the city's students became a crime and punishable by death after Pol Pot invaded the city. The teaching profession looked on as an instrument to spread lies, received unadulterated treatment, and then was dealt with appropriate [murdered] aggression.

The younger children were told that old family values were meaningless and in 1974, the Communist Youth League of Kampuchea came into full awakening as a useful force for Pol Pot.

> I'm quite modest. I don't want to tell people I'm a leader
> Pol Pot (Died in 1998 at the age of 72.)

During Pol Pot's later years, he saw a change in the city schools and universities, reemerging in the early nineties after the birthrate saw a steady increase. The children's attitude and former Cambodian spirit returned to respecting mother, father, and family values.

The adult population in the city, interested in rebuilding the city placed marriage and family secondary, so the birth rate among future young professionals, and tradesmen were less, because the new Phnom Penh was destine to come first.

# CHAPTER 4
## The Killing Fields of Phnom Penh, Cambodia

The visitors' reception center at the Killing Fields honors thousands of murdered Cambodians unearthed after the conclusion of the war. However, what the information does not show, because of bodies found throughout Cambodia, is that the American armed forces killed 750,000 Cambodians in their own effort to destroy the Vietnamese Army escaping into Cambodia.

The photographs from the walking tour in the Killing Fields outside the city of Phnom Penh, and the S21 prison in the city, depicts the suffering of the people in 1975. To understand today's Phnom Penh, it is necessary to relate that history, and too, to appreciate the contradiction and turmoil of her people at present.

> Cambodia possesses now the rights to look far into the future and everything for making a future construction is waiting for the Cambodian own efforts.
>
> Hun Sen

> Hun Sen has accumulated highly centralized power in Cambodia, including a 'Praetorian Guard that appears to rival the capabilities of the country's regular military units.' The former Khmer Rouge commander has consolidated his grip on power through a 'web of patronage and brute military strength.'
>
> Information from Wikipedia - The Free Encyclopedia

The Killing Field's visitor's center offers a tape recording of what transpired during Pol Pot's killing spree. During the walk, the tape tells what occurred at each of the stations with numbered plaques that correspond with the recording.

The Killing Fields of Cambodia, located 15 km southwest of Phnom Penh, is not a location every tourist who visits the city should see, but those who are of stout heart and sympathetic to the city's history.

A bumpy thirty-five-minute ride by tuk tuk over a not so paved highway passes through hamlets, depressed farming plots, groves of mangos, and industrial sites. The ride was pleasant enough, but I was not prepared for the serene setting surrounding this monument to the dead. I thought, would I find torturing devices and gallows in open fields. Arriving, I find a reverent area to the tens of thousands who were unearthed and memorialized.

Upon entering the parking areas, other tuk tuks and motorbikes had arrived earlier with tourists. Through the rusted metal gate, covered mounds of lush green grass bordered by swaying palm trees greet me with a welcoming motion to enter.

The same gravel used in the parking area creates walking paths that wind through the area with a respectful calmness. It presents a placid yet disturbing feeling on what happened from 1975 to 1979.

To the right front are numerous earth depressions marking the acreage from uncovered gravesites, now covered over with grass. Leaves blow over the dig, a startling difference for a false first impression I had two-months earlier.

The killings by sick-minded people capture the thoughts, touch the senses, and exposes feelings of the inhumanity of man. I think, be reverent walking from one section to another, and careful not to offend others with my camera.

Not sure what to expect from the silence

The first stop is at a small shed with three property custodians who politely greet and hand a pamphlet with a tape player and headphones for a five-dollar donation. Before entering the compound, one of the guards informs me about the tape player, and the 60-minute walk around the site. He says that the tape recorder will guide me from the first stop where the prisoners first made contact with their guards and points of historical interest, and then at each following stop the atrocities that occurred.

After the guard finished his presentation, and while adjusting the earphones, I see graphic photos of the prisoner's remains after they unearthed the graves. In a glass showcase are articles of clothing from one of the guard's victim, a respectful tribute to The Killing Fields dead.

The monument of skulls and skeleton remains, dedicated to the thousands who died here are in stark contrast to the tranquility of stone paths, and swaying trees.

Their last ride is inside a crowded truck

The first stop, called the truck stop, is where the prisoner's hell began. This allowed me to pause and contemplate the mind-set of the guards, as they were caught-up in a murderous rage from early morning through late evening. This stop after the people were trucked from the city was for some the final stop, because as soon as one or two came off the truck they were immediately murdered and their bodies pushed into the ditch.

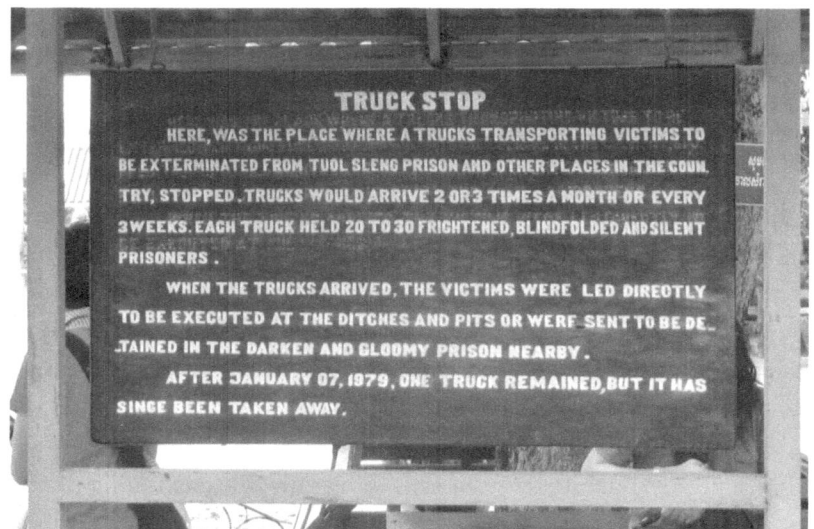

The Truck Stop was the first stop where some prisoners were immediately executed in a nearby ditch after they exited the truck. Others were tortured, and then within hours or days, murdered.

After stopping at the tool shed and sitting for a few minutes, the headphones detail a vivid link to the past, as a breeze calms my thoughts. I think, why didn't the prisoners fight back, even though they knew they were going to die? Then it hit home. I think, maybe the guards would just torture them even longer than killing them on the spot.

Around the rear of the camp, a six-foot high chain link fence surrounds a partially submerged swamp. In the background, 86 burial pits conceal the majority of the victims, still buried after the slaughter. Next to the fence, a solider sits quietly on a wooden chair separating the visitor from those still interred beneath the surface.

Because of religious standards by the Buddhist, there are no plans to unearth additional bodies. The Cambodian government and city leaders of Phnom Penh are respectful of the dead, and so they are [victims] left undisturbed, and guarded.

Some of the guards threw crying babies against trees

Following the fifty-yard path around the back end of the compound, and in the center of the grounds, additional depressions pay tribute to the victims' final resting spot. To the left, The Killing Tree stands erect where infants and babies were thrown against it until they died. Other stops before and after the tree tells how people died, and of the historical facts after the Killing Fields were uncovered.

The Khmer Rouge systematically and thoroughly removed thousands of inhabitants from Phnom Penh while destroying much of the culture and buildings, leaving behind a shattered city and a traumatized people. Hundreds of people, still lying on the streets had the nerve to fight back or were of political importance to the former government, were shot where they stood. The dead, many shot in the head, provide a futile testament to a rational society that was not part of, or prepared to accept their new jailors illogical thinking.

Inhabitants removed from the city were given a choice by the solders. They could work in the fields for 14 to 16 hour days, or were sent to The Killing Fields to be tortured and murdered. The ones who worked in the fields died from over-work, starvation, or singled out by children for being part of the former teaching profession. Pol Pot kidnapped the children, interrogated, and subsequently brainwashed them to turn on the adults, even giving up their own mothers and fathers.

Over 1,300,000 of the population disappeared

During the conclusion of the Vietnam War, Communist Vietnam invaded Cambodia and put an abrupt and final end to the Khmer rule in 1979. Democratic Kampuchea (Khmer: Kâmpŭchéa

Prâcheathippadey) the name of the Khmer Rouge (a forced and unnatural state of the Khmer Rouge).

The Khmer Rouge controlled the people during 1976 through 1979 while ruling the Southeast Asian country of Cambodia. Kampuchea was uncovered and then exposed for the butchery of millions of innocent people in Phnom Penh, and for devastating a culture. In 1991 the state was renamed Cambodia with support by the Paris Peace Agreement Conference, and reinstated by concerned citizens.

The horrific carnage of men, women, and children throughout the city and country was more than could be counted, yet figures obtained after years of research uncovered 20,000 burial gravesites.

Many of the deaths came from the deliberate starving of prisoners, and the general population dying for lack of food. An estimated 1,700,000 to 2,500,000 additional people died out of the total population of 8,000,000. With their deaths the quality of life and the mainstream of doctors, nurses, teachers, professors, tradesmen, artisans, and a majority the professionals, were wiped from the face of the city.

Thousands of women were tortured, raped, and killed during this horrific period, yet they still outnumbered the men during the post war years. The results would contribute greatly to the lack of new births for many years after, with an average age less than FIFTEEN years, or forty to fifty percent of the population.

After they were murdered, the prisoners were stacked to conserve space in one of hundreds of pits where victim's bones were discovered years later. Many bodies unearthed, had been butchered before they were thrown into the pits.

The guards would remove the spiny leaves from nearby trees, allow them to dry, and then use them to cut the throats of their victims using a sawing action to see the results.

Throughout the Killing Field's site, 129 pits were identified on the property, and of these 43 were painstakingly unearthed in 1980. The remains of over 19,000 people included men, women, little children, and infants. Separation of body parts and crushed sculls became mentally exhausting for the volunteers to continue as some quit, while others continued out of respect. There could be in upwards another 40,000 additional skeletal remains in the remaining 86 pits in the swamp.

Even during April 2012, bits and pieces of bones and cloth come to the surface after rainstorms wash away the topsoil. While all material and bones are treated with the respect due the people who died here, the staff wishes not to exhume any more bodies, but to leave them where they were buried.

Behind the chain link fence, 86 additional burial sites exists, but are too many to remove for burial so the area is guarded, and entry is not permitted.

The Magic Tree was used to mount a loudspeaker that played music. It helped drown out the screams and moans of victims being tortured and executed, and to lighten the guards state of mind during their killing spree.

The Killing Tree was used to tie children against as they were beaten, and used to throw babies against until they were crushed to death. The pit to the right served as the final interment of children of all ages. When the International community began their excavation of the site, the area was then covered.

Inside the three story high structure there are four glass-encased sides, displaying over 5,000 human skulls and thousands of bones stacked on wooden platform tiers.

Remains left from the mass murders of innocent people are the skulls, skeletons, and bits of torn clothing. One of the visitors asks me, how could any person treat and murder another person like this? I had no answer for her.

Their deaths helped to clarify the city's history

After visiting this historical site, I did not expect the dramatic harshness on touching history. Now I know where they died, but not their feelings. I think, it's difficult to believe that with all these people murdered here, there should have been more that could have been done to help them. Leaving the compound all I can do is look back in wonderment.

More children in the capitol of Phnom Penh live on the streets than any American city

One of the highest rates of mortality in the world occurs in Cambodia, with 200, per 1,000 deaths for children from the ages of one to five years. The majority of these children [abandoned] succumbed to malaria, diarrhea, hemorrhagic fever, and malnutrition. Additionally, intestinal worms, and a high rate of venereal diseases, were and still are a major factor as the children's frail bodies surrender to their environment.

These children live by themselves or as part of smaller cells with other homeless children. In a few short years, one or two may die due to environmental causes, raped, or taken off the streets and sold on the slave market. The remaining young survivors move on to other areas of the city.

# CHAPTER 5

## In 1975, the Tuol Svay Prey High School became the S21 Prison, Today's Tuol Sleng Genocide Museum

To the relatives' of those who died in the Tuol Sleng Genocide
Museum (Hill of the Poisonous Trees), this tribute is for them.

The location of the Tuol Genocide Museum is in a section of the old-town (Street 103, Boeng Keng Kang, Phnom Penh), 1/3 of a mile from the Mekong River, and 4.7 miles from the Phnom Penh Airport. Originally, it was one of the city's most respected schools for the middle class prior to 1975, but the education and friendly atmosphere changed dramatically on Thursday, April 17 of that year.

Photos of dead prisoners replaced student paintings of Buddha

A twenty-minute walk from the Silver River Hotel leads to the school's campus, and at the entrance, a black metal gate opens into a large inner court. Surrounding the courtyard stately trees and green manicured shrubs, and three, three-story buildings make for a beautiful entry. I'm not sure what to expect arriving inside the courtyard, but after seeing the Killing Fields yesterday, I am obligated to see the other half of history. Even though I know it was a place of incredible significance, I imagine objects of artistic worth for the time-period, with museum pieces of sandstone and clay elephants. I think, maybe I will see watercolor paintings, as I saw at an art gallery near the river.

Winding paths through the campus yard unites the buildings as the fresh scent of cut grass intoxicates the nostrils. I pause closing my eyes for a moment, picturing myself after cutting my own grass back home. The sensation of pleasure is misleading for it does little to prepare for the vivid display within the schoolrooms. The courtyard offers up an unrestricted feeling of openness, and reverence with springtime images, a fabricated notion of tranquility

After entering the grounds I read the visitors' plague, I think, how can people enjoy killing others? The grounds and buildings was a place of unspeakable horrors in 1975, but today I stand (awed) by the placid nature of colored ceramic brick paths. An average of 500 visitors weekly, many Cambodian and Vietnamese Nationals come to this school to see the city's horrific past.

During 1974, personal mayhem was the rule of thumb

French educated Pol Pot (19 May 1925 – 15 April 1998) invaded Cambodia and made Phnom Penh his headquarters. He began the genocide of the Khmer culture, haphazardly at first, and then systematically raised the degree of punishment to an art form.

[He] Pol Pot shut down the city and the schools, and along with the students and teachers forced them out of the city, expelling them and their families to the rural areas as slave labor. Along with them, thousands of citizens in Phnom Penh were forcibly marched to the outskirts of the city, and died within months.

Immediately, Pol Pot headquartered in the city, transformed the Toul Sleng Campus and the buildings into a torture facility, ideally suited for his fanatical appetite for inflicting death on the helpless, with a zealous unsurpassed anywhere in the country. With few exceptions, his uncontrolled taste for pain and suffering during four-years of horror was unmatched throughout the world.

On the first floor of the main building is the museum, containing, not sculptures of Buddha or student reports, or watercolors of elephants, but devices used to cause pain on people, and that was the surprise I had not anticipated; it is a bit disconcerting.

Entering the largest building on the first floor, and inside the first two rooms, hundreds of black and white photographs of prisoners hang behind glass encased displays on three walls. The photo to the left is of a photograph of a (terrified) human with eyes open, and blank of any emotion, and to the right another photo of the same person, the eyes closed, lying dead on the concrete, blank of any emotion.

The word "prisoner" to describe the people held captive at S21, is appropriate, because descriptions as inmate, criminal, detainee did not fit, given that the people held here had any hope of ever escaping.

The placid scene today is quite different from how it looked - sounded then. A hundred prisoners at any given hour cried out from the inhumanity of guards dealing pain, and as the carnage increased, their dead bodies smoldered in the courtyard, swelling in the hot Cambodian heat.

Two of the three buildings flank a stately and groomed courtyard, yet cannot reflect the dark atmosphere prevalent in 1974.

This view is from outside a prisoner's room on the second floor. Some prisoners could not see from their rooms, but heard the cries for help and mercy that echoed throughout the courtyard into the late evening.

Life as a prisoner, at the Hill of the Poisonous Trees

When people arrived at S21 they waited in line to be photographed and then were required to tell the guards their life history. After the initial autobiography (that was filed away), every man, woman and child were forced to strip to their undergarments and everything they brought with them was confiscated.

Inside the school, many were held together with iron bars that ran through ankle shackles in large rooms where they laid on cold concrete floors. They were forbidden to talk to one another and were severely punished if they did.

Every morning at 4:30 am the prisoners' day began, when they were told to strip as the guards check them for anything they might have acquired at night to commit suicide. During the four-years, prisoners would obtain any item to cut their own throats or wrist to bleed to death.

They were allowed two meals per day consisting of four spoonfuls of porridge and cooked rice and a soup made from boiled leaves. Any unauthorized drinking of water was dealt with by severe beatings of wooden or metal rods unless they asked the guards first.

Little medical treatment, performed by the untrained guards would force the prisoners to drink human urine or eat human feces. Living conditions were so hideous that many developed skin diseases, ringworm, and rashes that covered the body.

Guards had instructions to deal with their prisoners as they saw fit, but had to keep in mind that over 1,000 to 1,500 additional people arrived every week - they had to make room for the new arrivals.

The guard's laughter and prisoner screams was like a horrible symphony

Four months after they took power in Phnom Penh, the Khmer Rouge transformed the school buildings in August of 1973 into a secret prison, and out of 150 such prisons in Cambodia this was the worse. The school was changed into an interrogation center, adapting the building's interiors into rooms for torturing prisoners, as was the courtyard. Larger second and third story rooms changed into smaller units housed some prisoners, while areas on the ground floors were modified into smaller cells, separated by brick walls and entrances. Some rooms had front doors while the majority had open fronts with ankle chains that anchored the prisoner to the opening, or shackled their feet to the rear of the cell.

Both men and women enclosed behind electrified barbed wire had little hope of living through the week. The windows (if a prisoner had one) were coved with iron bars that permitted them to have fresh air, but the down side allowed them to hear the painful cries from prisoners in the courtyard during torture.

It is impossible to imagine the pain and horror of being there, with no hope, and knowing that without a doubt you were going to die. Of the 30,000 murdered only six people were found alive of the four-year period, and when the Vietnam soldiers arrived in Phnom Penh the survivors' related horror stories of their stay in S21.

Prisoner rules posted on campus grounds was strictly enforced. The question arises, who was that someone who took the time to construct the sign and hand-paint the rules in two languages.

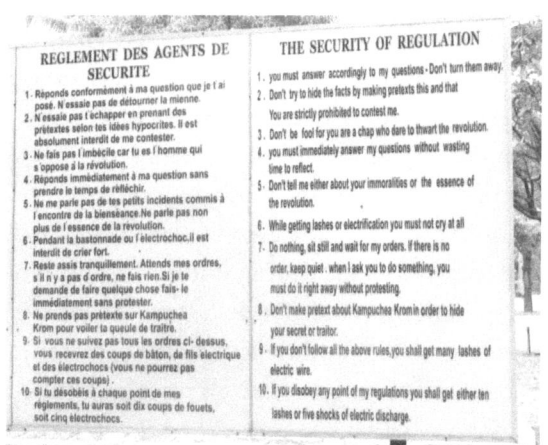

Guards made the atypical torture, typical

Pol Pot's lunatics carried out insanity with no regard for human life or suffering even overwhelmed their own children with the same brutality. Averages of one-hundred prisoners were murdered every day.

Many decaying bodies, stacked and rotting in the courtyard, and some burned to death were found throughout the campus grounds and in the rooms. A few bodies, still hanging upside down in water-pots, became an ordinary routine, making what the guards did more horrific and bizarre.

The certainty of hell for thousands

From 1,000 to 1,500, men and women occupied the facility at any one time, and were subject to random beatings and torture throughout the day and evening. In addition to farm and homemade implements, fire was also applied, and in some cases burning of the entire body while the victim was still alive was customary.

Some estimates of the people murdered were 17,000 to 20,000, but after officials located a few former women and men guards who fled the area in early 1979, they placed the figure closer to 30,000.

A sign in the courtyard stated that it was against the rules for any prisoner, who while being tortured, to cry out in pain, for rule, #6 forbade them to do so. Additionally, children administered homemade Rabbit-Pellets during the victims' torture, so they would stay awake and not pass out from the relentless beatings. It is unknown what the green pellets were made from, but it kept the prisoner conscious during hours of unbearable agony and torture.

Children were taken away from their parents only to be tortured and later killed, and then after the screaming stopped the corpse of babies and teenagers were all tossed on piles of other lifeless bodies in the courtyard.

The equipment and items used for torturing prisoners was not elaborate, but well constructed as this slanted table, used for electrifying prisoners, and the water box attests to the 20,000 or more deaths.

At the entrance to each four by five-foot cell, chains secured the prisoners to the floor. Some rooms were constructed into individual cells with brick walls and fronts and a doorway.

The interrogation room where prisoners were subject to questioning and torture. Inmates gathered together to stand endless hours in groups awaiting to be questioned and then later taken to other rooms inside the compound for torture, or hung outside to be whipped.

 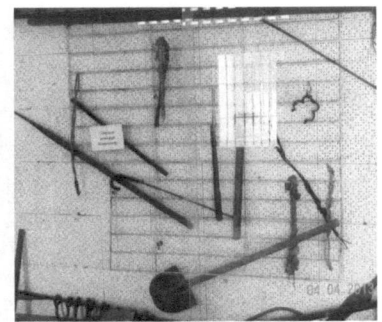

The Gallows. The original school's physical fitness rack that students used to exercise turned into a prisoner's hanging rack. Prisoners had their hands tied behind their back and hung while beaten. Pots below them, full of (filthy) water became the vessel to invert the victim's heads into, until the prisoners were conscience.

Showcase of tools for burying the dead, and other items to inflict the maximum amount of pain on the prisoners.

After the Vietnamese Army discovered the prison, the six remaining prisoners reported the daily events and tried as best they could, the horror of watching family members and friends tortured and murdered, and of their own pain. A prisoner mentioned how a few people set afire while alive screamed from the pain, and then later the stench of blackened, burnt flesh filled the compound from their twisted, shrunken bodies.

A majority of the victims came from the Lon Nol regime that included most of the former soldiers, and every government official. There was no distinction between Buddhists or Catholics, bankers' or tradesmen either, if the Khmer Rouge thought you were a threat, you had to be eliminated.

As the years progressed, the party leaders of the Khmer Rouge became paranoid and turned on its own leadership. Throughout the country, thousands of adamant party activist and their families were brought to S21 and murdered as well, believing they were going to overthrow the present leadership.

Vietnamese soldiers, 150,000 strong plus 15,000 Cambodian exiles entered the city of Phnom Penh on January 7 1979, and only found 40,000 residents roaming the streets searching for food and water. The Vietnamese soldiers found the city 80% destroyed except for the flies, rats, and mosquitoes that inhabited a decimated capitol, and a river with bloated bodies.

The Vietnamese Army on entering the S21 prison saw inhumanity at its worst and as the clean up began some hardened soldiers who viewed the site became ill and could not stay in the school grounds and help.

Among the photographs discovered on the walls and from files, surprisingly, more than a few pictures were uncovered of foreign captives from France, Australia, England, and the United States.

The school reopened in 1980 by the People's Republic of Kampuchea as a historical museum to the public, and over the years thousands of people have visited it and learned about the hardship of the people who made history.

The Killing Fields, The Tuol Sleng Genocide Museum, Pol Pot, and the Khmer Rouge played major roles in the reshaping of today's Phnom Penh that change the city for decades to come. Phnom Penh still carries those days throughout the city, not as a badge of courage, or medals for heroism, but a simple sign in the grass that might read, we may not remember those times, but we can't forget the memories.

# CHAPTER 6
## How the Shadows Survive in a City of Many Lights


From childbirth, up to four-years of age the children living in Phnom Penh's rural areas have a higher mortality rate than those in the city. If they survive those first few years, they are forced by their parents to help with the farming. When they grow older and with a failing crop production, the mother will send her children to the city, begging for food.

Now on their own a child begins life on the streets, and for days does not return home for lack of money. These shadows of the city roam the city, standing for hours in front of shrines, restaurants and city parks.

City officials are aware of the increase in children joining the streets, but cannot or worse will not protect or feed them. The children are more than the system can absorb, plus city officials do not have the means to calculate how many children live in the city, and so the government does not do anything for them.

Lacking care at home, many children leave longing for attention, and end up on the streets forming small groups. The children amble aimlessly through the city, and for some become snared in sexual traps set by those visiting Phnom Penh, or by adults who run houses of prostitution. They entice the younger children with promises of personal care and food, or forcibly take them to areas where older children live in sex. The unfortunate ones face a life of sexual exploitation with older adults and a daily life of degradation, or worse, removed from the country and sold to the international slave traders as early as six-years old. For each virgin child, traders will pay from $400.00 to $600.00 each.

Visiting Phnom Penh may be hazardous to your wife in Europe

An internationally recognized area for child prostitution, 11 kilometers from Phnom Penh, was the high profile brothel district of Svay Pak, employing over 300 people. It was an active center for child prostitution, and due to the concentration of foreigners in the area, and pressure from international organizations, all operations of child seduction and trafficking closed the brothel in 2005.

The underlying causes for child prostitution stems from an ignorant and closed-minded society, widespread poverty, intellectual indifference, and a corrupt judicial system. A report from the United Nations states; over a third of the prostitutes [children and teens], have AIDS and HIV. Despite this alarming fact, parents sacrifice their daughters, sisters, and friends into this hell, and by doing so the rise in venereal diseases exploded throughout Cambodia and Vietnam. With no help from the public or government officials to curtail or halt the spread, visitors leave Phnom Penh for home infected with the virus as well.

When world officials located the young children in locked rooms, they were living together with older boys and girls in insane living conditions, and starving. City leaders aware of these areas did little to nothing to restrain the practice. Not to say that tourist seek out these dens of depravity under the watching eyes of the government, but little was done to enforce any laws broken. It is safe to say that these travelers add a small amount to the local economy, and if any of this money flowed back to the city officials, I can only speculate. [Ed]

It is unfortunate that a few families prostitute their own children, forcing mom and dad to make a decision to give their children and the child's future away to this lucrative business. Offering them in exchange for money to support the remaining family members is not the norm, but it does happen.

After the parents are paid for the children they will never see, the mother and father are left with financial compensation that only last for a few months. It is a final cruelty for the family, but sometimes those who are left, even the grandparents, this is the last and only hope for them to eat.

Pol Pot Guaranteed help was not forth coming in 1975

Today's children of Phnom Penh are an indirect causality of the Vietnam/Cambodian War, because the majority of the adult population murdered in 1975 left the survivors to begin a new society, with the assistance from China and Vietnam. Those teens and adults, less than 50,000 in the city, married, and as their children grew older, they married, and continued under the most terrible of conditions.

The people's plan was to survive in a city torn apart, and because Pol Pot destroyed the currency, and left little food, immediate self-help was unavailable to sustain the simplest way of life. The thousands that did survive depended on the Vietnamese Army to aid in their recovery.

Since the period from 1980, the city had nearly an impossible task to rebuild a damaged economy with a crucial shortage of tradesmen; placing on the thousands who remained a mammoth yoke of responsibility.

The older girl of five children watches over her younger brothers and sisters. The heat of the day is difficult for one child to survive, but to care for four others is asking too much from her innocence.

A mother caring for her sick child that may succumb to malnutrition continues her watch. In 2012, the average percent of children from 0 to 14 years of age in Cambodia was 31% and in a country over 14 million people, many of the children die before age five.

Foreigners seldom pass through this part of town, and of those who venture off walk by, apparent to the grief around them, yet oblivious to the pain caused from it.

In one of many poor sections near the city's government buildings boys enjoy their shadows. They are a reflection of the thousands of homeless that are not seen by the government.

Life expectancy of the population in Cambodia less than 57 years

Phnom Penh's average population is well below twenty-seven years of age, plus approximately 24,000 children, 13 years and younger, live on the streets with an additional twenty percent increase every year.

The plight of the Cambodian is quit evident

⌉ The July 2012 population in New York City was 8,336,697

⌉ April 2012 population estimates put the number of homeless children in New York City at 17,247.

⌉ The July 2012 population estimate for Cambodians was 14,952,665,

⌉ Over 2,000,000 people live in the capitol of Cambodia.

⌉ The average age for both males and females for Cambodians, is 23.3 years.

⌉ Sixty-five percent of all Cambodians are under the age of 25 years.

⌉ Estimates are 700,000 children 5 to 17 years of age in Cambodia work, plus 230,000 drop out before finishing school.

⌉ The National AIDS Authority (NAA), informs us that 80,000 to 125,000 (8.3%) children in Cambodia and orphans, are susceptible to the AIDS epidemic.

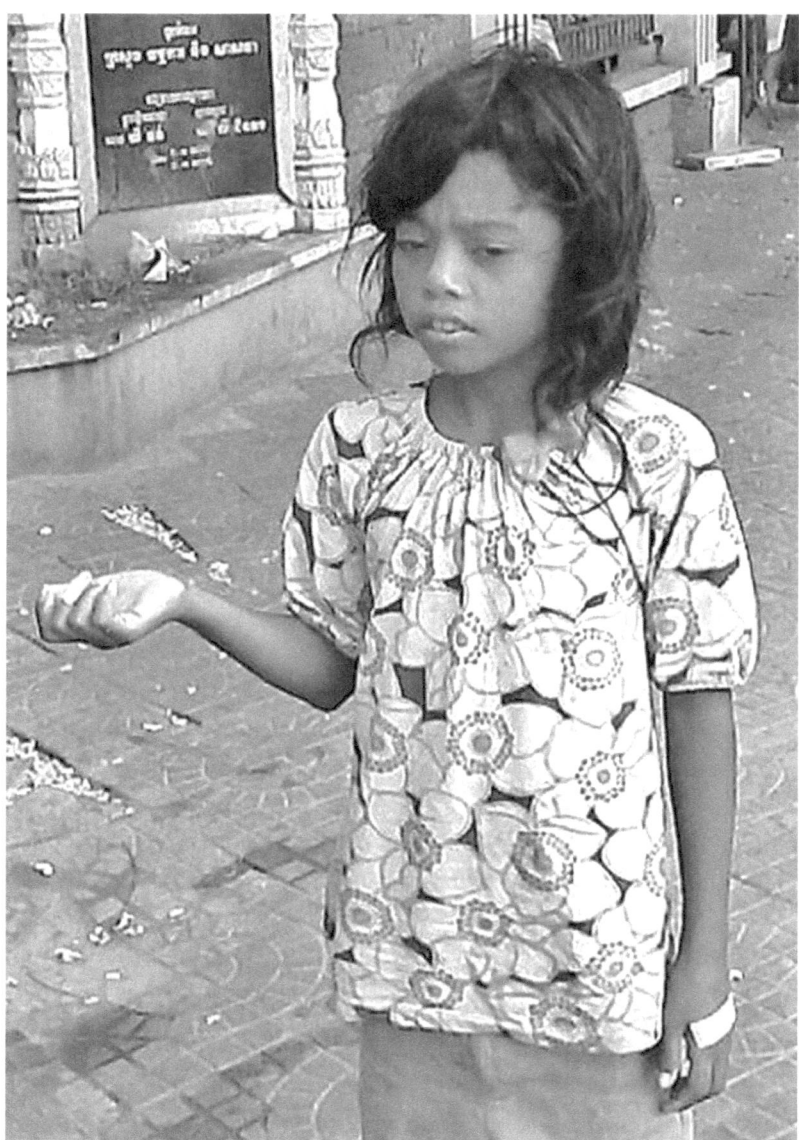

This seven-year old girl, wearing a soiled dress, has been following me for three blocks, begging for money. She is dirty, infected, and has a sour smell that surrounds her like wet wool.

It doesn't matter where I walk, this girl tags along, or moves to block my way, and any street I cross or busy road I put between us, she eventually ends up alongside me. I offer her a fresh bottle of water, but she turns it down, only wanting money.

The problem is any money I give her, would not be enough, and her insistence would only continue. I don't want to be rude, yet I must be firm, because she won't leave. When her sister comes to join her, I convince them to pose for a couple of pictures. After two shots, she realizes her futile attempt to continue; they smile and then walk away.

Streetwise teens will steal from or kill younger children for money

Children in Phnom Penh who have evaded predator adults are fortunate, yet, rummaging through the city rubbish or in the gutters isn't that much better. Most times they live with older children for protection, but that only last for a year or two. To graduate into the older gangs, the rules are harsh, and dues need paid to the pack leaders. It isn't always about money, yet the initiation can be brutal for a thirteen-year old boy proving himself prior to acceptance.

These older teenagers have learned another lesson, how to harass unsuspecting first time tourist visiting the parks. Foreigners that come to photograph the riverboats, and the Royal Palace, should not fear for their life or their wallets, but sadly, they are not immune.

Street gangs do not limit themselves taking money from children, but will confront and intimidate foreigners into giving them a few American dollars. Tourist do not feel remorse saying no to a five-year old girl, but it isn't as easy when you are confronted by teenagers.

I have not seen teenage girls with any boy, so I might expect two things have occurred. One, they have been abducted and are part of the slave trade and used for prostitution, or two, they have found an older male suitor to care for them, as with males from Vietnam and China.

# CHAPTER 7
## The Expense of Feeding a
## Child or Help a Developing City

Children living on the streets in the United States comprise a conservative estimate between 500 thousand to 1.6 million. A disturbing number of the highest estimate are students living in America without a permanent address, and that includes those from pre-school age through the 12th grade. Over one-million educated boys and girls did not have a permanent address in America for the period from 2010 to 2011.

In addition to this staggering figure, millions of homeless men and women strain the government's resources as cities across America struggle with both gender groups. The homeless are less visible in the larger cities than smaller towns, because they tend to concentrate in abandoned buildings, under bridges, and slum areas of the city where authorities are unable or unwilling to locate them.

The homeless roam the streets looking for handouts, and to protect what few items they have, carry them in plastic grocery bags, or in shopping carts. Violent incidents on the public are few, yet some homeless carry clubs and knives for personal safety. In addition to this self-defense attitude, the more disturbed have assaulted pedestrians due to self-anger issues.

Towns across America have their share of the homeless teen asking for handouts or money so they can purchase drug. These teenage boys and girls prostitute themselves to stay alive, and for many this is the only avenue they have to obtain drugs. Police are stretched thin with major crimes, so consequently, the hundreds of teens on drugs, overdosed, or die in the arms of friends.

On a larger scale than the United States more children die in Phnom Penh from drugs than any city in America. Adding to this figure are those who die from starvation and murders.

The U.S., tells us that government programs, to help the homeless, are in place and working, yet have 'no intention to help the children with food or shelter. City and state officials lack the courage to address this problem with the compassion it deserves, especially with the available finances that could be diverted from other programs.

The United States has it's own Paradox Banks or Taxpayers

The government's financial effort for the homeless fails in comparison to the growing national economy. In 2009, the National Science Foundation, received 6.9 billion dollars. Additionally, $644 billion went to Social Security, $408 billion for Medicare, and Unemployment/Welfare/Other mandatory received $360 billion. During this same fiscal year, the U.S. government only spent $2.9 billion dollars to aid the homeless, and the greater part went to adult programs already in place.

Washington also allocated billions of dollars overseas to help countries with their financial debts, sending billions to governments who oppose us to purchase arms.

A secret deal, known only to a select few in the Treasury Department and the Feds, gave without question or conditions, 460 billion dollars to Well's Fargo Citibank, J. P. Morgan, 2nd Bank of America under the TARP program. Additionally, over 14 billion dollars, loaned to over 400 small banks is still 'owed to the U.S. Treasury under the TARP program. A Puerto Rican bank is still in arrears for $935 million, as is the Zions Bancorporation (ZION) bank out of Salt Lake City that has not repaid half of the 1.4 billion given to them.

A few of those financial institutions, who have not repaid their debt, proves there is no conviction or legitimacy to Congress's idea of financial reality. In fiscal year 2013, $23 billion went to foreign aid and $14 billion to train foreign military armies to provide them with state of the art weapons.

Millions of dollars are given to the constant flow of illegal immigrants to help them in America, to obtain illegal citizenship and jobs. Additionally while the sick,. displaced veterans, and the mentally challenged continue to enter a life on the street.

One out of six people go to bed hungry in America

The figures change by the minute, but as of Saturday, September 19, 2013, every ten seconds a child died from hunger below the age of five. At the end of today, 21,000 will die for lack of food and water. In the United States 17.5 million households were deprived of the basic amount of food for this month.

Globally 100 million people are homeless and starving

One out of every four children is under-weight, and every ten seconds a child under five dies from hunger. The world has the capability to feed every man, woman and child, yet government intervention, corrupt government officials, wars, and the lack of adequate distribution, more adults and children will continue to die.

The tonnage of food we as an affluent society waste is 78,301 tons, yet the global market could only provide to the hungry, 16,258 tons of food. Worldwide for the people living in extreme poverty, they live on less than $1.25 a day, while Americans waste more food collectively as families, restaurants, farmers, and grocery chains discard rotting, and expired food, than any other country on Earth.

*When a poor person dies of hunger it has not happened because God did not take care of him or her. It has happened because neither you nor I wanted give that person what he or she needed.*

Mother Teresa

How America and Phnom Penh deal with the homeless

The majority of children living in America, compared to Cambodia have a better opportunity to score drugs and get something to eat than their counterparts in Phnom Penh.

A major difference is separated by an affluent society that can do more to feed and house the homeless, than Phnom Penh that struggled to maintain its fiscal budget for 2013. The ca[itol of Cambodia had a disappointing economic growth for 1997 and 1998, and in 2005, but rebounded with new international countries establishing an economic foothold in Phnom Penh. While this news benefits the city's plan for expansion, the poor continue to struggle day to day. The end result is more children will starve in Phnom Penh than any city in America.

> *We think sometimes that poverty is only being hungry, naked, and homeless. The poverty of being unwanted, unloved, and uncared for is the greatest poverty. We must start in our own homes to remedy this kind of poverty.*
> *Mother Teresa*

An underlining economic growth in both cities comes from the teenage drug trade

The rural areas of America are not immune to an increasing drug problem, as the epidemic invades all class elements and ethnic groups of our society. No matter how affluent or poor the teen, or their color, the ease to score devil smoke, *Crack Cocaine*, depends on the right amount of cash at the right time.

In Phnom Penh, to purchase glue to sniff is difficult, but not impossible, because it only takes .50 to $1.00 US to buy enough to escape the frustration of living on the streets. As early as seven years, they develop this habit, substituting their need for food, and for these children to move to hard drugs, they become more aggressive, stealing from other children.

Today's American family (saddled) with work related stress and teenagers living where parental concern lacks direction, find living on the streets with their peers easier than fighting with mom and dad. American homeless children, group together to provide acceptability to one another, the herd mentality. Grouping together as cattle is similar in Phnom Penh, yet on a larger scale. Twenty-four thousand homeless children are as flies around the faces of the tourist. They are a constant annoyance with no food, no place to stay, and without hope.

The plain indifference of the people in Phnom Penh toward the children

> *Phnom Penh's homeless adults and children*
> *are not privy to the social services offered*
> *to the thousands living in America.*
> Anonymous - Phnom Penh

When tourists continue giving the children money, the child equates this as an immediate incentive to continue begging on the streets. Due to this success, the mother will have more than one of her children circulate as teams, increasing her chance to make more money.

Soiled clothes and dirty faces the children attract the attention of dinners [myself] to give them money, so they will leave. After a few minutes the mother whispers to each child to move to another section of the outdoor restaurant. There are more tourist in the city.

Individually, the young girls have more of a chance than boys have because a flower print dress, cute appearance is more conducive for tourist to give them money. If they can make just enough, less than a dollar U.S. they will purchase shoe-polish or glue, and go somewhere quietly and get high.

Unfortunately, these children are not the visually enticing faces one sees on national television. The innocent looking with chubby faces and clean dresses girls on brochures are not the typical homeless child of Phnom Penh. The crusted dirt on clothes and hands are real, and owned by the children of the capitol of Cambodia. They walk without shoes and most cases are infected with AIDS.

An emasculated young girl sits quietly getting high on the glue from a bag, purchased for .50 (100 Riel) from one of many dealers. Her weakened body and the effects from inhaling fumes have shortened her life by five years.

The out of focus photo is indicative of how city officials see this growing problem among teens, and do not help. Given time, this girl will soon disappear eliminating the decision by city officials for the girl's future.

A 2005 survey taken with 2,271 street kids, 16 percent admitted to sniffing glue, and with a growing street population of teens, the number could be 3,700 to 4,000 in any given month. These boys and girls roam freely on the city streets without the intrusion of shopkeepers or the police who will not stop them.

The park across from restaurant row is not a safe place to rest, so this older teen sleeps at the Wat Penh Shrine Park, one mile away from tourist and gangs. Watching her for a couple minutes, I think, *where did she come from, and does she live somewhere near?*

The Dragon Boys [don't play with stuffed bears]

Across from the Silver Pagoda and the Royal Palace, couples from Asia and local families enjoy the sights and calming sounds of the park, and a river flowing to the Delta. It is a pleasant park where tourists come to dine and spend their vacation money. Unfortunately, teenage gangs also frequent this serene area of Phnom Penh.

Four boys swagger by foreigners suggesting they should be wary. Unaffected by their gang mentality, a little girl sits nearby, playing with a stuffed bear. A five-year old boy walking aimlessly on the grass stares at Japanese tourist hoping for money. The girl and boy not bothered by the teenager boys continue playing, but tourist hurry to another area of the park.

Another gang - rough, ugly, and killers, *(The Dragon Boys)* ride motorbikes through the city doing snatch-n-grabs. The tourist industry, suffered in 2014, due in part to small item thefts, and became the subject of NGOs [non-government organizations] reporting to Cambodian National Police. Motorbike gangs follow tuk-tuks and snatch the bag or items they can grab in an instant, and then speed away through traffic.

The well organized gangs operate unchecked throughout Phnom Penh, as major embassies reported their tourists were robbed, and a few received personal injuries. This cannot be verified, because the police do not keep actuate records.

After returning from Cambodia, my friend Emily ask me. "Why didn't you travel around America and report on the homeless children living on our streets?"

The reason simply put, I tell her, "homeless children in Phnom Penh don't have the advantage of walking into a shelter to eat a hot meal, or sleep in a comfortable bed like in America."

She says, "we can't help all the homeless, but isn't it enough to try to …?"

I cut her off, and with an abrupt tone, I say "It's not up to me to tell the public what any city in America could fix, but will not." She says, "Why doesn't America do more?" I say, "Emily, the United States doesn't care about the homeless, but in Phnom Penh they do, by letting them die …" I stop talking.

She is silent. We finish our pizza.

American cities offer places to escape the summer heat and the winter cold for the homeless, and with unlimited efforts in tandem with private corporations could provide additional capital for food whenever they cared. That we do not help our homeless was the reason I didn't focus on America, because what difference would any report make to shore up a crumbling program.

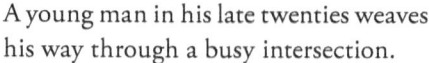

A young man in his late twenties weaves his way through a busy intersection.

This man had one mission, to sell belts that he might have stolen from a street-side vendor earlier in the day.

As I move aside to avoid eye contact, Phnom Penh's dark shadow passes me; his eyes tell the story of a lingering fight with the black devil.

Did anyone talk common sense to Hitler, Stalin or Pol Pot

After a destructive Vietnam War that overflowed into Cambodia, Paris educated, Pol Pot destroyed many of the temples and killed most of the 60,000 monks, leaving alive 3,000 to tell their story. The monuments to depravity from the Killing Fields, and the lust for murdering other humans at S21 only became known to the country after Pol Pot's ouster. In a couple of years the world's news media, now aware of the horror of the atrocities from his murderous philosophy, then reported it with graphic detail. The legacy from Pol Pot is still evident and (shockingly) visible today in Phnom Penh. It is not on the it is not on the hotels and restaurants but on ancient city temples, on the faces of old women and men, and the crippled. It is on thousands born who survived the war.

Cambodian's corrupt government agencies, struggle to stay honest

It has always been the government's (internal) conflict between providing funds to rebuild the city or help the citizens. Phnom Penh believes they are doing the best they can for the general population, taxing the citizen to support the police, firefighters, and social services, as well as setting aside enough finances to run the government. However, corrupt government agencies attempt with such programs do not (by any stretch of the imagination) help the farmers, and the children roaming the city. Their efforts to help those less fortunate [the homeless child] receive a token amount of the services available, when 15 million children globally died of starvation in 2013.

The immensity of worldwide humans' stagers the conscience thought at a figure of 7,297,686,958 as of this writing, and that 1.3 billion live on less than $1.00 to $1.25 each day is criminal.

The United States has 324,238,954 people, and with a child born every 8 seconds globally, these people need fed. Should we as a society fund the city or care for the citizens, and the less fortunate? To rebuild cities, and still care for the population is a daunting task, yet governments must concentrate on basic human rights; a priority for every nation to address, and not just in America and Cambodia.

As this report proved, the city of Phnom Penh will not, by government mandate, care for the homeless, the crippled, the thousands of children walking the streets, and 90% of the population ... poor. No dictatorship does. Minimum care is provided without dated medical services, forcing the pooron their to the streets and on their own.

*Power does not corrupt. Fear corrupts ...*
*perhaps the fear of a loss of power.*
— John Steinbeck

# CHAPTER 8
## Stung Meanchey Landfill, Home to Thousands

In a southern district of Phnom Penh, there is a region called Stung Meanchey, where families and children make their home and place of "business." It is an area outside the city, local government officials are not too proud to have seen by outsiders. The low-income housing (landfill/slums) is acceptable to city elders as a dumping site for Phnom Penh's garbage, but the families living there it is not.

Looking out the third floor hotel widow at six in the morning, and with the temperature at 84 degrees, I might consider staying in the comfort of an air-conditioned room, but not today.

The Stung Meanchey Landfill is not a tourist attraction your tour guide would suggest you visit, but Berta talked to a tuk tuk driver and asked if he would take us there. We found what he described about the landfill tempting enough to hire him to drive us there tomorrow, and so we agreed to his $15.00 rate.

Later during breakfast, I ask Berta. "Are you ready for today?"

She says. "John, I'm glad we are going there together. I hope we can talk to a few children."

Berta is a twenty-five year old missionary student from China, and as we head to the landfill, she tells me she speaks three languages. She was a great help yesterday obtaining the services of our tuk tuk driver. .

The Stung Meanchey Landfill miles from Phnom Penh, is far enough to give Berta and I time to talk over what we would ask the children. Hundreds of children live in such deployable conditions it is unthinkable to imagine people believe they live well.

America's Great Smokey Mountains National Park

Within the great American states of Tennessee and North Carolina are the <u>Great Smokey Mountains National Park</u> known the world over by thousands who yearly visit the mountains. Travelers come to see the beauty of graceful mountain ridges, feel the cold brisk air in winter, smell colorful wild flowers in the spring, and photograph the abundant wildlife throughout the year. In the fall the hills come alive with the changing of leaves rejuvenating tourist with their magical beauty. Remnants of the Southern Appalachian Mountains, this is *America's most visited* national park.

One hundred acres of garbage that children walk through

Phnom Penh has its own "Smokey Mountains," due to the burning mounds of waste from the Stung Meanchey Landfill. The fumes of methane gas billow up from the constant fires and at times block out the sun with fluttering pillows of grayish-yellow smoke. Falling on the children the noxious mist clings to their faces, as they pick through each new truckload of trash.

Throughout the year and specifically during the monsoon season the area surrounding the dump becomes an infested swamp where rats and mosquitoes thrive. The water from rotting waste washes down from the mounds of trash collecting in black pools, expanding the swamp where the children play.

Working for as long as there is sunlight, adults, and children sort through the debris and food waste from the city. Those who are directly behind the back of the truck are the first to get new items. They are also the first who are hurt and covered at the rear of the truck by the refuse or if the truck backs over them.

The security guard has informed us not to take any photos of the buildings, but as the rubbish truck passes us, the long road ahead leads to buildings with smoke rising from the burning trash.

The large buildings, miles away, may be used as apartments, or an incinerator. The property is much larger than I had anticipated, and due to the length of the road from the entrance, the landfill must be immense.

Approximately 2,000 people, and 600 hundred children, live on the 100-acre Stung Meanchey Landfill, and pay rent to the landowners for the privilege to stay on private property. They live in huts made from torn rugs, cardboard, broken plywood, and plastic covers collected from the trash arriving daily.

The families and children endure the danger from broken glass, serrated metal and rats. Sorting through the expanding compost from two-million people, trucked every twenty-four hours, the families are never without trash, or the opportunity for one more valuable item.

To say the children are pickers denotes they are fussy, but indeed are not, for they are trash gatherers, looking for anything worth selling or to trade. Many of them do not wear footwear, and walk through the mud and rubbish, with cuts, bleeding toes and heels. A few tie cardboard to their feet or wear over-sized discarded shoes. Those who stop to sort through the trash walk out coughing and spitting nauseous phlegm. Wiping her mouth and nose on a dirty rag, a five-year old girl ask her mother for water.

Rats run rampant throughout the landfill feasting on a diet of sun-baked garbage, and at times biting at the child's hands as they separate the torn clothes from the vegetables. Hundreds of the younger children sort through trash and food waste others did not want as their contribution to the family's meal for the day.

At key points throughout the landfill are buyers wearing boots, clean clothes, and designer sunglasses waiting with cash to purchase bags filled with old and torn clothing.

The scenes described were found on the hundreds of pictures on the Internet, but not allowed to enter the landfill to take my own photographs, I relied on those organizations that did; the pictures of dazed faces, some smiling, are real.

The majority of the pickers at the dumpsite came from the city of Phnom Penh where they could not find steady employment or begging was not enough to support the family. Others journeyed to Phnom Penh when they too could not find enough work in their village, and ended up at the Stung Meanchey Landfill as well.

Where are your government papers?

Arriving at the entrance to the landfill, Berta, the driver and I stop by a half-open gate that blocks the entrance side of the road, while the exit side is free for traffic to pass. Berta asks the driver to go around the gate, and that is when we notice to our immediate right a thatch-roof guardhouse and a security guard sitting inside with his feet propped up on the ledge, sleeping.

The guard awakes, and (immediately) waves for us to stop. Frantically, he is pointing at the driver to pull off the road. We stop, and our driver gets out. Berta looks at me and then goes with the driver toward the guard, asking him why he stopped us.

Berta is the first to speak. "Hello, my name is Berta. We would like to go to the landfill," she calmly says.

I am out of the back seat and walking to Berta and the guard with my camera.

The guard looks at Berta and I, and says to Berta. "Show me your official entrance papers." The guard is direct but not rude.

"What official papers?" Berta asks with a smile, knowing we did not have anything but our passports. She turns to me for advice. "John?"

"I don't think he wants to see our passports," I whisper to Berta.

Berta and I look at each other on what to do next.

"Excuse me sir, no one told us that we needed papers to enter the landfill," I say, thinking my presence would somehow sway the guard's viewpoint.

The guard is a bit more assertive. "It's the (government) papers that allow you to go to the landfill. Can't let you enter unless the city gives you permission." The guard stood his ground.

"You mean we just can't drive down the road and take a few pictures?" Berta interrupts.

"No, you have to have papers from the city just to enter here," the guard says. This time even more direct, sensing the three of us are being aggressive.

I step away while Berta continues talking to the security guard in Khmer. She motions for me to come. "He's calling his boss for permission to drive down the road just to take a few pictures. I think we may still enter."

A security guard stands his ground, telling us to leave.

I ask Berta. "Tell him I'm writing a book about the people living here, so maybe outside organizations may help the children."

The guard telling us that his boss said "no" we could not pass or take pictures of anything we see, and we must leave immediately. I have the impression he might and would call other more stern authorities to handle the problem if we do not.

What we did not realize, until returning to the hotel, was one important item. If we had told the hotel manager that we were going to the landfill he would have told us to present a written request to the local authorities, or the U.S. Embassy for documents to enter the landfill.

There is a moment when Berta pleads our case that the guard looks like he will allow us just to drive down the road.

Berta continues. "We would like to take a few pictures from a distance."

The guard is distracted, so I continue taking a few photographs of buildings in an open field down the road.

The guard finishes talking on his walkie-talkie and notices me taking pictures. "Boss man says you have to have papers to go into the landfill and you, no more pictures. No exceptions." This time, his tone is to the point. Pointing to us to turn around and leave, he keeps telling us. "You must go. Go, now. Turn around - leave! You are not allowed to enter or take pictures."

Not discouraged, Berta did find out the original landfill's address. Berta bows to the guard out of courtesy, and we leave having one additional chance, to see another landfill. We take a couple of quick photos and see the guard vigorously waving his hand not to take any more pictures. I sense he may come over and physically be more direct so I tell the driver. "Go!"

Driving away I say to Berta. "Thanks for all you did, trying to get us in," I say, "I know you tried your best, but I didn't know about any government papers we needed."

"Oh, that's okay, I'm sorry too. Might have been exciting to see what goes on down that road." Berta opens a bottle of water, and after a sip, we head for another landfill. She leans over and whispers, "I thought the driver should have known, but maybe he has been instructed not to ..." She pauses, not finishing her comment.

I know what she means.

Lessons taught at the landfill by Frenchmen bearing rice

One notable organization, headquartered in France, has located a school and other family facilities less than one mile from the landfill. They are the largest and most effective in supplying some measure of education, and meals to the children.

While the younger children learn basic schooling, the older ones receive career training in fields that could help them later in life. Every day before school, hundreds of children receive a *free breakfast*, plus the families are provided with financial aid.

The organizers realize the families can't always afford the cost for their children to attend school, so they also supply rice as an incentive for the children to stay in school. Regrettably, some families take the rice but still send their children to the dumpsite, while other children attending school will go to the landfill after classes.

Blowing the whistle on the city elders for not taking the lead

Cambodian and specifically Phnom Penh officials ignored the deplorable living conditions at the landfill, because it was financially burdensome to support the families, or improve their huts, they invite outside organizations with the necessary funds and training to handle the problem for them.

Unfortunately, few International groups or local volunteers are able to supply the minimum requirements, leaving gaps in medical care for hundreds of needy children. The French organization while applying similar efforts in other countries with food, teaching aids, and medical care, can only provide basic support to the Phnom Penh problem.

I ask Berta, "What languages do you speak."

Berta is taking pictures on the right side of the tuk tuk (French word remorque), and tells me. "I speak Chinese, American, Korean, and a little Cambodian. My English is not so real good, but I try."

"Wow! " I say a little surprised. "You told me you spoke other languages, but I didn't know which ones. You've been very helpful, talking to the guard. By the way your English, is very good."

"I did my best," she says.

"Thanks, Berta. I know you did, but the guard was just doing his job," I say.

She says, "I wanted to see the dumpsite too, but I didn't feel comfortable alone. Thank you for coming with me."

It should be easier to gain entrance to the old landfill, but we may have a problem with these guards for I was told not to take pictures inside a shopping center, an abandoned train station, and an hour ago, at a landfill.

Cambodia hid from the world, the conditions at the landfill, and of the people dying

This landfill conveyed hopelessness when it was operational, and at its height, over 120 trucks visited this 24-acre site. Day and night, they added to the trash and eventually it was, *100-foot high* in places. Mounds of trash, rotting food, and debris from years past, overflowed in peoples yards.

During the landfill's peak, adults and children worked endless hours, gathering items they could resell to others at the dump, or outside on the main highway. Many of the children living there were homeless, abandoned, orphaned, or sent there by their parents who came from nearby villages.

They were subject to communicable diseases, and the danger of infected cuts that without proper medication could kill a young child. Part of the dumpsite's legacy, roving teenage gangs harassed the residents, adults who dealt in child trafficking, the putrid toxic waste, and even death was part of their life.

The truth to close the 44-year-old Stung Meanchey landfill

When families living at the landfill became severly ill from the toxic waste, local NGO's and the international press stepped in. City leaders were then forced to halt operations and orderd to close the site. The landfill was a symbol of Cambodia's failure to care for their citizens.

In time, Deputy Governor Chrean Sophan replaced the original landfill with seventy-four acres of (newly constructed) Choeung Ek dumpsite. The attention to a modern facility counteracted the negative publicity, of the Stung Meanchey. Oddly enough, the new landfill is located near The Killing Fields.

From the Bayon Bakery to a dirty place where children live

After fifteen minutes, our driver pulls off the road, and says, "we have a flat, but I can fix it in a few minutes," he says, "you both can get out and rest in the shade."

His friends, an elderly couple run a small stand selling tires and assorted glass bottles filled with gas. This is where Berta and I get out of the tuk tuk and set on two wooden crates under a large colorful umbrella and drink our water. It is in the high eighties, and riding over miles of potholes, it's good to sit still.

We are in an area of sub-standard housing between unproductive fields of dying fruit trees, and abandoned shops. "Berta, are you hungry for pastry?" I ask, noticing a bakery across the street.

Berta notices it too and says. "Yes, John, that's one of the famous bakery chains in the country. I've eaten their cakes and pastries many times, and they are delicious."

"You mean they have donuts?" I say looking across a busy highway, and wanting a sweet bite of Heaven on Earth.

"They have many shops around the city and the country, and yes, they make their own donuts." Berta says with a smile.

*The Bayon Bakery*, a famous bakery chain in Phnom Penh, just happens to have a store across the highway. With a storefront of orange, yellow, and red paint on the building and awnings, it is an invitation I am happy to accept. Walking across the busy highway, dodging motor bikes, I make it across, and turn around giving Berta a thumbs-up … she smiles back.

Standing in front of the store and looking through the window, I'm amazed on the selection of cakes, breads, pastries, and donuts. Entering, I'm greeted with the typical Khmer's *Sour Sdey*.

Looking in one of many showcases, and a little wide-eyed, I finally settle on three huge pastries filled with fruit, totaling 75 cents. I ask for one with apple filling, a pineapple, and for myself a gooey, chocolate center overflowing down the side. Returning, and within a few minutes, we are enjoying our fresh baked goodness. The chocolate center of my pastry is dripping on my cheek, we laugh like kids.

A ride back to history and despair

After twenty-minutes, the driver turns onto a side street for half a mile, leading to another gate. It is higher, and with two uniformed personnel standing behind the entrance, this could be a wasted trip. We hesitate, until our driver waves at the two guards. They smile and motion for us to come forward. Hopefully, we may enter to take pictures, and see for ourselves the living conditions of the families still here.

Berta is first out of her seat and talking to the guard. They inform her that we may go to the other end of the landfill, but not through these gates. She turns toward me, shakes her head yes, indicating we can go to another section of the landfill.

Berta in front of a security gate to the main entrance of the landfill, asking the guards for permission to enter.

At the old landfill, there are several heavy-duty plastic covers concealing, acres of old trash, while in front flowers grow.

The guard suggests we could take pictures if we followed this road through the back alley to the other side of the landfill.

On the edge of the landfill a small community of huts house hundreds

With new directions we head down another dirt road, passing huts built like "cookie-cutouts." During the monsoon season, the first floors of these huts will flood, yet the residences do not seem to care.

In front of a few huts, people are selling children's clothes, cooking utensils, cigarettes, and candy. Even though these huts are poor by most standards, the closer to the edge of the landfill, the living quarters are more like sheds. It is obvious that there is a tier society, even at this abandoned landfill.

The tuk tuk squeezes through an alleyway to the end of the southern boundary of the landfill.

In this area of meager dwellings, I'm surprised to see dwellings constructed of wood and metal, while nearby brick buildings are under construction. At the end of the dirt lane, there is an area to park, where Berta and I leave the driver to mingle with the families.

This landfill has not been used for years, but it still reeks of rotting food, and fossilized debris beneath the surface. Even though, we came prepared with our surgical mask, the smell stings our nostrils and throat.

Facing the edge of the dumpsite, Berta and I see something different from what either of us imagined.

Berta says, "I thought there might a few people living here, but not families. "Yeah, I say, "I didn't think there would be so many either."

"Yeah, I see it too!" I say, surprised. "I don't see anything new for them to pick through."

Just off the edge of the landfill, two story dwellings for families are under construction, with cinder block and brick, while corrugated metal sheeting is used as a temporary roof. To our left, workers stop and watch us with some hesitation. I look away, thinking, *I hope they are just curious.*

A new brick building for the locals living at the landfill. The people still throw their rubbish outside the back mixing it with the trash left from past years .

The Stung Meanchey landfill was not a happy place for man or rat

Paths wind through the landfill, covered with twisted trees growing through the trash and weeds that give testament to the conditions of the past. Walking past a decaying tree, bats hang from distorted branches, for this is their home, and are undisturbed by our presence.

The reason city officials closed this dumpsite was not because the area could not sustain additional garbage, but because the international community forced them, due to people becoming ill. During the closure, the city planners had to find a new, larger area to handle the growing amount of garbage arriving from Phnom Penh, and a better way to (dispose) of the trash. The capitol's new 30-hectare dumpsite, Choeung Ek, was the answer.

A surgical mask cannot prevent the stench from a dead pig

The equipment from the old landfill that covered the garbage here is now used at the new landfill, so after 44-years this site is left to decay. A sour and stale heaviness lingers knee high, and only moves when an occasional breeze flows over the trash, stinging our eyes.

Twenty-yards to either side where we are walking, a debris field undulates beneath the trash, blocking a direct route to the top of the mound. Plastic containers, discarded clothes, boxes, broken glass, and jagged metal pieces stick through the weeds, making any safe route across hazardous.

Before navigating further through the trash, I snap a shot of a pig lying in the muck. It may be dead, but because it is too close to one of the huts, it may be a pet or an upcoming meal. A few feet away, I spot a dead rat on top of the trash. I think, *what did it die from*, and walk around.

Is this pig a family pet, this week's meal, or just dead lying in the muck.

A rat lying in the garbage. It too could not survive this place.

Author with mask. It helps to breathe yet the stench is intensely noxious.

Half way through the debris field, Berta notices the ground below me is sinking. She yells out. "John, be careful there might be water below the plastic bags!"

Too late, my right foot sinks on what I think is solid earth, only to find that the cardboard box sinks into the water. Now I am standing with two feet, sneakers, socks, and pant legs up to the ankles in the foulest black ooze I ever saw.

Reaching the other side, I'm concerned about the thick pasty water and what remains in my sneakers. I think, *maybe I should remove them - then what?* My socks are drenched, the pant cuffs are black, plus the sneakers smell, and I don't want to touch either. I can do little more than slosh ahead.

Adjacent to the closed landfill, new buildings under construction will be part of the apartments for the residents who stayed.

Dead trees and shrubs on top of the largest hill and while very little grows, bats and a three-foot lizard claims this land as their own.

Some grass and weeds are sprouting through the dirt and trash, but it is a meager attempt by nature to <u>reclaim the land</u>, for sections here are too spoiled. At the top, there is a huge mound of dirt covering the garbage left after the landfill was closed by the city, and then filled over by bulldozers.

Standing at the top of the hill, overlooking a barren valley floor, Berta says, "Oh my John, I can't imagine how large this dumpsite must have been."

Overlooking the land below, a fabricated house sits in the middle of the dump where trash once burned. The makeshift house from sheet metal, strips of wood and cardboard are nailed to the sides, and a chimney with smoke rising from the center of the roof completes this picture. Outside the hut, trash is burning a few feet from the house, smoldering as if someone is clearing the land making the place a home. Neither of us see anyone on the grounds, so it might be that he's at the other end of the landfill, or inside, out of the heat.

An outlet pipe running from underground, flows with infected black water, and while striking in black and white, in color the green growth is visually unsettling.

Berta stands in one of the few areas of green shrubs and weeds. The trash left on both sides of the path and on the hill gives evidence to the amount that was here before.

A still open pit shows the depth of trash that had been uncovered. The bottom is another fifteen feet lower, making this hill 30-feet in high.

An elderly couple with a shy son; a day in the Cambodian Sun

The landfill is peaceful enough today, but try as I can, I can't envision what it was like years ago as trucks and bulldozers weaved through hundreds of adults and children as they searched through the garbage.

"John, I've seen enough, and the smell is too much for me." Berta says, after twenty-minutes, "it smells funny."

"Yeah, you're right, the smell is getting to me too." I say while removing my mask and wiping my nose and mouth of the sweat, still tasting the heavy moist air that settled around my mask. It was a mistake to remove my mask. {Ed}

Berta says. "It must have been horrible for the children."

"Even these pictures," I say, "can't do those people justice."

Enough is enough, I think, *we must return to the city*. Looking over to the tuk tuk, the driver is still sleeping in the back. I think, *how many times has he seen this depressing sight*.

Returning back on the same path, we meet a family; two adults with a young boy pushing a rickshaw that someone else found useless. Berta stops and asks them where they are going, and what are they doing with the rickshaw.

Berta says to me, "They found the rickshaw and are taking itl to another family on the other side of the dumpsite," she says, "they may fix it and use it to haul debris or for transportation to the city.

The father and mother are just under five-feet, and thin from lack of proper food, plus the boy with his head down, stands a few steps to the rear; he is meek and quiet and looks twelve or thirteen, and undernourished.

I ask Berta. "Ask the mother how old is her son."

Berta asks the mother, and then tells me. "He's seventeen years old, and doesn't talk much to people." Berta says, "he hasn't had much schooling and doesn't eat much either."

The lack of a proper diet has stunted his growth, yet his facial features are smooth as a boy four years younger. His demeanor is placid and obedient, as are the majority of children living with their parents. The mother goes to the side of the cart while the son pushes from the back as his father pulls the cart. They leave, not saying anything more to us.

A family who lives at the landfill transports a rickshaw up the hill to a neighbor living on the opposite side of the dump.

Blue-collar workers to the rescue

Crossing the swamp an hour earlier was difficult, but now we are looking for a safer path through the same field. Berta and I are trying to avoid our first mistake. So we walk along the bottom edge of the hill. This seems like a better idea, it is not.

Berta is kind-hearted, smiles, and says, "Let's try closer to our first path instead."

"Okay, sounds good to me," I say, carefully turning around.

Workers on the other side of the pool notice our hesitation and motion for us to cross in another section. One worker is pointing to an area a few feet from where we are standing, where the ground is solid, and dryer. On the other side, I wave a thank you to the construction workers as we walk to where the tuk tuk is parked.

A few of the construction workers notice we are stuck on the other side of the marsh, and point to a dryer path through the bog.

At the edge of the dumpsite the living conditions are a mix of old shanty's and new block buildings. The huts are raised one story, leaving the bottom of the hut for storage while the floor above is the living and cooking quarters.

Berta calls to the driver, and tells him we are ready to leave. He smiles, and then motions for us to get in so we can head back to Phnom Penh, telling her it may rain soon.

The more distress homes are at the edge of the landfill, while further away on either side of the dirt road are better units of wood and stone.

Berta asks. "Do you think they are satisfied with their life?"

Berta, the driver and I leave with our water, cameras, and memories and head back to town. We are wiser from the experience.

Berta is quiet until I say. "Berta, you know how fortunate we are not to live here, and only visit this place?"

She pauses for a moment, and says, "yes, how lucky we are to return to our hotel for a hot shower, and meal."

I say, "when the driver said we should leave because of a storm coming, he was right." It begins to rain, a steady rain cooling the air, and settling the dust. I ask Berta. "Is this how these people bathe, only when it rains?

Berta tells me. "I was thinking the same thing a minute ago, and felt bad that maybe it's true."

I think, *is it selfish to feel good?*

Back on the main road, heading to the city, I ask. "Berta, how do you think these people live from day to day?"

She settles back on the cushion, thinking of a logical answer, and then pulls her mask down. "I don't know John, but it's not easy." She pauses, "and I didn't expect to see what we just saw." "Did you?"

I look at her, and think, *what answer could satisfy.*

# CHAPTER 9
## Speak Loudly for the Children; They Have no Voice

Many inner-city residents put their trash and garbage on a collective heap awaiting pickup by one of hundreds of wooden carts. The practice is unusual in most of the city's more affluent sections, but in the areas away from tourist, it is common and an accepted practice.

A one-man cart circulates through the city picking up each pile by hand and then drops them in a larger pile at another location. Eventually, city trucks drive through these areas [wider streets], load it and haul it to the landfill.

Near one of the main roads, shopkeepers stack their trash on the sidewalks, awaiting removal by a city worker. From the odor, this pile has been on the sidewalk for a few days.

After Wednesday breakfast, I take the bag of plastic bottles collected for the last three days, and at the corner of the street, place them on a pile. I Think, *It will be interesting to see if I can spot the person rooting through the pile, and if so, will they take the bottles.*

At the end of the street, two boys are playing while an elderly man sits cross-legged on the ground looking in my direction. I remove three bottles from the bag, placing them on the pile. The boys rush across the street to scoop them up, and run back to the old man. After placing the remaining bottles the five-year-old boy rushes back to claim them. The old man and his grandsons tie the bag of recyclables and then leave. As they walk away, one of the boys turns and smiles. It was a good start for their day.

Sleep my baby, mommy watches over you

After breakfast at the Silver River Hotel, I ask the desk clerk where I can find the seedier side of the city. She gives me a city map, and points to the sections of the city that are the poorest.

Six blocks from the hotel, a family of five camps outside a Buddist Temple. It will be a temporary address, for in a few days they will be told to leave. The mother and father sleep on hemp mats, as does the older son, while a three year old girl stands at her mother's feet.

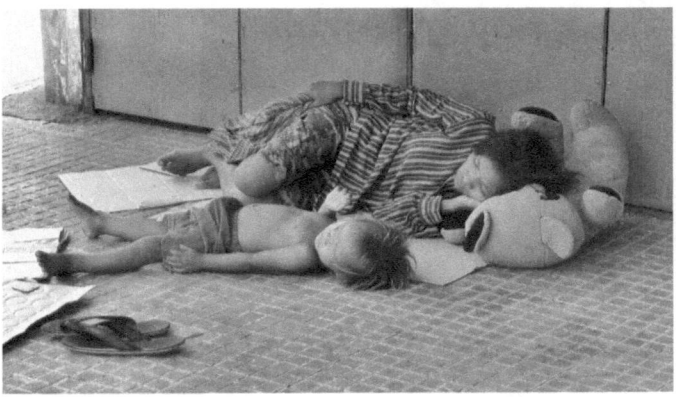

Mother and daughter sleeping in the heat of the day.

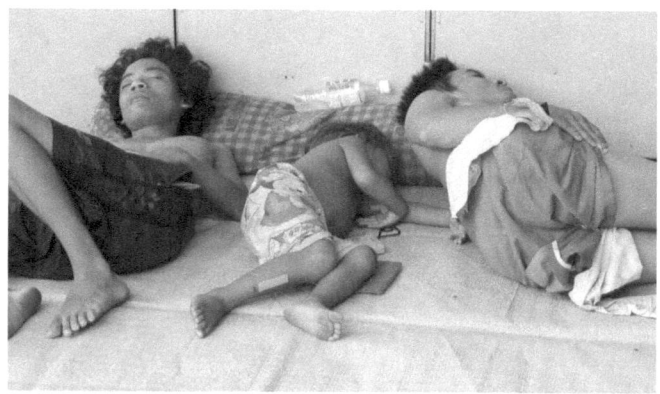

A family living on the streets of Phnom Penh. The temperature in the 80s and the humidity over 70% only adds to their discomfort.

The three-year old could use the extra bottle of water more than I could, so I hand it to her. She takes it and then gently shakes her mother's arm. The mother sits up and then opens the bottle, giving it back to her daughter, and then resumes sleeping. The three-year old with a forced smile and *wide-eyes* says a silent thank you. A quiet gesture, but enough for me to backtrack to locate a market and buy more water and food.

Returning with water and fudge cookies, I place them in front of the mother. Her three-year old girl shakes her mother's arm once again. The mother, sees the meager gifts, and then opens the bag of cookies, the water bottles, and gives them to her children, not keeping any for herself. The <u>family's faces</u> <u>reflect a hard life</u>, but appreciative of any help offered to them, and this gesture contributes to a portion of their day.

The son is still asleep, while the father and the two girls eat the cookies, and with the mother, all have a little respite in a day of heat and dispare. The bottles of water are still chilled and with the cookies, give a little help to one family. After a few minutes watching, the sorrow of their life sinks in.

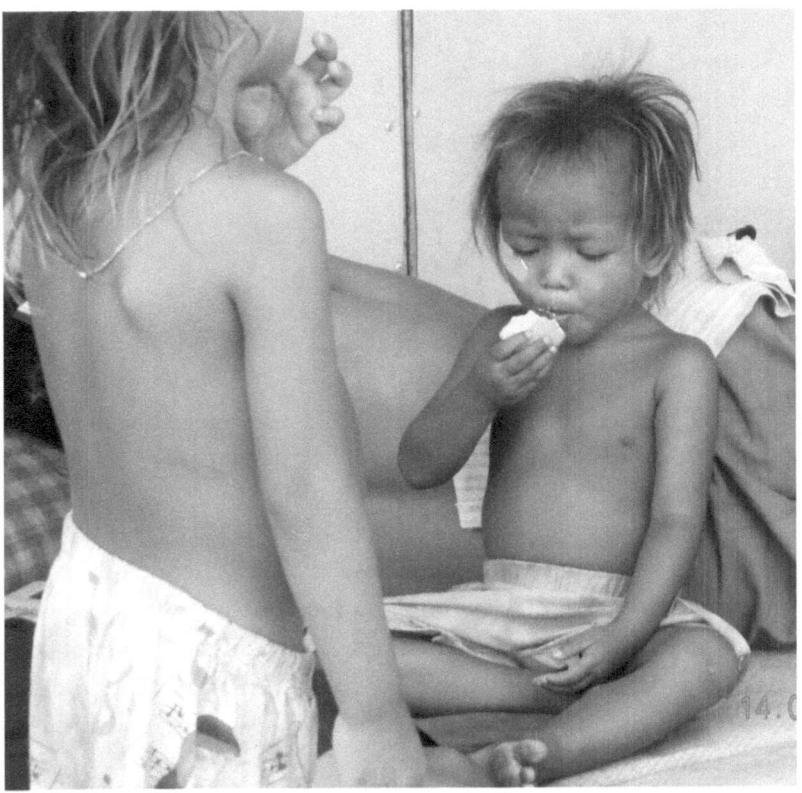

Eating pastry given to her, may be the only meal she will have today.

This family is typical of the city's less fortunate, and not because of where they live, but how the city allows this to happen. During my time walking the alleys and side streets, many families camp where they can find shelter, or anything they can use to construct a place to stay.

Watching them, I see in the eyes of the mother a futile attempt to continue feeding her children by herself, yet she is accepting it with grace. Her family's future is doubtful and uncertain yet, she continues to keep them alive, and I would like to believe she is telling them, *Everything will be good kids.*

It is a depressing sight to see an entire family so poor and wanting, yet the redeeming quality is that they are together and not separated, and her children are not walking the streets. I say to myself, *too many of the children living on the streets don't have food*. I can't feed them all, but God, someone should!

The mother and father look on while their two girls savor the fresh water. One of the girls will die within the next three years, and neither mom nor dad can stop it from happening.

The young and old share the alleys and sidewalks

On the other side of the street a man in his forties, wearing metal rim glasses, sits in the middle of the sidewalk, shuffling pieces of paper like playing cards that he picks from his worn leather sack. He tears them into smaller pieces, and scatters them at his feet. I take a couple of pictures but he looks away, unconcerned at my attempt to make him the cover photo for Time magazine, so I dream. My last full bottle of cold water I set at his feet, but he continues tearing up the paper, not looking up to acknowledge my gesture.

A lone man sits on the sidewalk, sorting through bits of paper like playing cards that he systemically tears into smaller pieces. He has a protective attitude while doing it.

The girl seems lost on what to do next, or where to go, for anything more is mentally beyond her understanding. She is a sad child, and ignorant of a better life.

Maturity comes from staying alive on the streets, it is called curb wisdom. Alongside his right side are an empty tin cup, a plastic container, and a worn leather satchel. I think, *there might have been some food in it at one time, but maybe not.*

At the end of the street, a forty-year old man sits cross-legged on the sidewalk, with a look of humility he pauses allowing me to take his photograph. Exhibiting a chin goatee, heavy eyebrows, and whiskers on either side of his mouth, he is a homeless street character, and one I think comes here regularly, because he is expected to.

Immersing into a reality unlike anywhere else is Asia that few tourist see, it is unlikely I will find anyone who is truly happy, but the streets have a way of hiding one person with a dream. Maybe this man hides that dream.

How do the homeless go on without losing all concept of reality, and not realize hope could be a few blocks away? The answer not to try, lies in their eyes that have seen too much of the streets to continue.

Thus far, I have seen children as young as five fending for themselves, and in every venue, and with all the miles, I never saw any sort of concerned endeavor, any meager effort, or (honest) attempt by the government to help.

How ironic that a city boast a rise in tourism, entice foreign capital, and apply a flourishing city budget toward new private and commercial construction, and leave behind the dejected and despondent poor.

# CHAPTER 10

## How Children Learn to Live on the Streets or Die Trying

The streets of Phnom Penh teach the children the unforgiving reality on how to survive the city, an <u>ordeal that is a harsher</u>, albeit, a wiser form of learning process than in school. And with this knowledge comes "street-smarts", their unofficial rulebook.

Attaining this unfriendly realization comes from disappointments and the proper method on how to beg. It will improve over time, yet it is Oh so necessary, and requires a strict adherence to unspoken laws. Flowery words cannot be used to explain this tormented life, but in reality it is simple, learn the way, learn the streets or be left behind.

Four children roaming the streets with dirty faces, and big smiles. One is shy, while the others take poses for the camera.

Mother with two babies in a cart with recyclable cardboard and containers.

The Bassac Block Housing Apartments

Of the many slum areas in Phnom Penh tourist seldom see, the largest, oldest, and most disgusting of all of them, appropriately, is known as *The Building*, It is a sprawling high-rise where hundreds of families live in open rooms.

The make-up of this complex is part of the government's official records that contributes to the growth rate of people living on the streets for 2013 at 25%. At year's end, 105,771 people will be classified as slum dwellers, a sizeable increase over the 2012 figure of 85,807. In the capitol of Cambodia 25,100 families dwell in city slums.

Many poor sections in Phnom Penh were built so close together, they share rooftops for hanging clothes, and after it rains, one three-story building's roof drains water onto the adjacent two-story. Some buildings are divided by a narrow walkway on the ground level, separated by a small courtyard, where each family's assortment of bikes and wicker baskets are stored.

The appeal of mixing deep-fried pork, motorbike exhaust, and boring days.

The cooking of deep fried pork fills the air from sidewalk cafes as fresh vegetables in a fire blacken-pot emanate a (very) distinctive fragrance. Today's sidewalk aroma mixes with today's meal along with neighborhood trash.

The streets have their own distinguishing characteristic as the sounds of horns from tuk tuks, scooters, and laughing children playing with little dogs, fuse together the smell of rotting cabbage, and motorbike exhaust.

A few blocks down St 110, off Norodom Blvd, a young man rest on a makeshift wooden bed of discarded wood planks. A block away two men under a large umbrella play chess, as a woman waits for them to finish the game.

In the center of the street, a man rakes garbage on top of a commercial dumpster, searching for something suitable to resell. His effort is to dig down as deep as possible with a simple wooden stick, as vendors continue throwing discarded trash and rotting food on top of an overflowing dumpster.

Taking a wrong street, European tourist pass an area they did not want to be in, as a young man balances himself on a garbage dumpster.

Local vendors sell cheap to hundreds

In a quaint section of Phnom Penh, is a neighborhood crowded with local businesses selling cigarettes, chewing gum, and children's flip-flops. However what makes these couple of blocks different are the lean-tos', huts and tents of friends selling more than a few basic items, and if one listens, the bartering over rice, and bananas.

This part of the city sits between streets 13 and 15, with crowded housing, and streets crisscrossing with an open three acres in the middle for parking. Surrounding the booths are lights circling the area, enabling the vendors to sell past sunset or until each vendor is sold out. This is an open-air market, long established for many years that grew from a concept by local people to sell their goods to other locals at reasonable prices.

Two enclosed markets, *The Russian Market* and the *Central Market*, house vendors inside while on the adjoining sidewalks, tourist venture for their slice of Cambodian culture, but here, the vendors are in tents and wooden huts.

A street side market in the poorer section of the city sells fruits and vegetables brought in from the rural farmers.

A vendor pulls his cart through crowded city streets filled with cans and bottles for recycling while on top are bags filled with torn clothes and rags. He has a labor-intensive job, but is one of the fortunate few who own a cart.

While the capitol's plan to increase tourism and local expansion moves forward, market areas around the city, only receive a token amount of the benefits. So when rural farmers have a poor growing season [one cycle] the produce supplied to the city would notably be curtailed. Unlike the capitol that can purchase goods from abroad, and pay higher prices if warranted, local vendors live day to day.

On the streets of the city, some sleep, others die

Sitting outside a Buddhist temple, three women watch a man lying sick on a crude wooden bed. The others watch the children, a two-year old, and a younger child, with another, a shy older boy sits at the foot of the bed with his mother. Wearing simple dress attire to cool them from the heat, the talk is about the man inside a makeshift hut, who is of concern.

Three women caring for their children, wait for the man inside the shelter to succumb to his illness.

The women are at a loss to help the man inside struggling to stay alive.

*Without health, life is not life; it is only a state of languor and suffering - an image of death.*
*Buddha*

Twelve minutes after three the afternoon of April 14, today's walk leads me to another unfamiliar street off the Monivong Boulevard. I think, *do I have enough water?* Each neighborhood has its own mini store, and vendors selling water, *so I should be okay*, I think.

At the end of the boulevard, a young man sleeps on a cot on the sidewalk alongside a temple wall, with his umbrella casting a cooling shade over him. Hanging from underneath the umbrella is a worn cotton bag with a colorful print of hearts and sunburst, something a child would keep when they ran away from home. This older boy, if he did run away from home or if his parents abandoned him at an earlier age, is on the (unforgiving) streets living day to day. His life is not pleasant, yet when he sleeps, that alone, distances him from reality.

A young boy sleeps under a torn umbrella. There is no sign of any food, only one empty plastic water bottle.

Wooden pallets and blue plastic covers are home to a homeless trash collector. His home secured over many years has been accepted by the locals, and is known as the man who collects plastic.

Two men have made this structure a permanent address in a lean-to against the side of a building. They have an abundance of personal items within their sleeping area, denoting they have been here for some time.

Many homeless males, females, and children living without parents, camp outside temple walls, where the environment is emotionally safe. People in Phnom Penh are spiritually close to Buddha, so it would be a sin to come in conflict with the homeless and their religious beliefs.

> *Have compassion for all beings, rich and poor alike,*
> *each has their suffering. Some suffer too much,*
> *others too little.*
>
> *Buddha*

Common among people living on the streets is a wood constructed lean-to that has slatted wooden strips as a bed, supported by four-corner post and a slanted wood or metal roof facing up to the front. It's enough room for two people or a mother and two children to sleep. Most of these huts are similar in design, suggesting that they are made and sold, either to order or at a place where one can buy them at a set price. Some are against walls, or between buildings in a vacant alleyway, while others are on the sidewalk.

Milk and fresh vegetables are not major ingredients of their diet

Due to a lack of vegetables and fruits, it is difficult to know the age of the majority of the people in Cambodia between 20 to 38 years-old. Most of the homeless spend a major portion of their day in the brutal sun that turns the skin leathery, and they do not regularly consume fresh water and meat.

A prime example is a sidewalk vagabond, with dark curly hair, gritty face, proper food and water plus the street years has aged him more than normal.

This once strong and healthy teenager, has been worn down by the (streets) of Phnom Penh, and now crushes soda and, beer cans to fit into his black pouch.

*A normal Cambodian meal generally consists of a light soup with vegetables, and pork or seafood, a mixed salad in a separate bowl and strips of carrots and onions. The staple and main dish of fish is served with white rice. Deserts consist of fresh fruit or sticky rice, with hot tea. This meal is not the norm for the majority of the people.

Man in front of his hut, crushing cans for recycling. His friend inside is making something to eat. Teamwork is essential, but these two have it easier than many that are on their own.

Bon Toms are the Cambodian equivalent of the Mafia

Across from the Royal Palace, alongside the Tonle Sap River, is a beautiful park with exercising equipment for the children, a pavilion to sit and enjoy the river, a small Buddhist shrine to pray, and a breathtaking view of the river during sunset. Even with this tranquil setting, <u>Phnom Penh has it crime</u>, and it starts with the atmosphere teen boys bring with them.

The *Bon Toms* is not a name of a new clique restaurant or an evening bar, or a shopping center, but older male teens in Phnom Penh. For those younger teens who do know, they are a group of males that will rob, rape, and murder the younger kids on the streets. These older middle-class teenage [gangsters] rule Phnom Penh streets.

April 11, four teenage boys circle their territory in the park, looking to harass locals or the tourist. For the next ten-minutes, the boys surrround an older man and his wife and then (talk) them out of a few dollars. What the tourist don't know yet might suspect is that these boys may use force if necessary.

It has been reported that some homeless and street teens will spit, curse and throw stones or bricks at tourist who don't give money, so offering a little money may detour personal harm. Local police are aware of the danger to tourist, unfortunately, the Bon Toms come from families' with (strong) political connections to government officials, shielding them from the the law.

Four teenage boys are part of the Bon Toms, a gang with political connections. They are part of Cambodian's equivalent of the Mafia.

On a Friday morning the Bon Toms roam freely through the park intimidating tourist just by their presence. A woman who is followed by the youths hurries across the street to the crowded park near the Royal Palace.

A security guard leans through the window watching a woman prepare her noonday meal with bits of pork and vegetables. I don't know if the two know one another, but he's not saying anything to make her stop.

Birds pick bits of dried bread off the sidewalk, as traders barter

An area of the street is a collection spot where trash and garbage accumulates over time. One carts contents, scattered on the sidewalk, attracts birds and rodents.

Facing west on street 228 toward the intersection of Pasteur Street there is a one-story government building on my right and a communal structure to my left. In the alley between the two buildings, the sidewalks are piled with trash, and overflowing from the curb to the street forming an unsightly mess. Even with the surgical mask over my mouth and nose, the odor emanating from this area is offensive and leaves a bitter taste in my throat.

To the right of the street a man sits cross-legged on his newspaper with a cloth cushion and plastic bags. The more personal items are close to the man's right side, and along with his bike. He sits with the two females, maybe one his wife who during her walks collects recyclable plastic and metal bottles before returning to her husband.

Coming toward me, yet seemingly not noticing my presence, one of the women carries her bag of food and other personal items.

Relax and enjoy the view of the Mekong Delta River

The Tonle Sap River flowing into the Mekong Delta River originates eighty-miles upriver from the Tonle Sap Lake at Siem Reap. It flows one mile down from the Royal Palace Park to form the main artery of the Mekong River, so notable in war movies, and history specials. Floating restaurant and hotel boats pass local junkets in opposite directions showing another side of Phnom Penh paradox.

On the Tonle Sap River, across from the Royal Palace, there is a public park where tourist and locals come to relax and enjoy the openness away from the confines of a crowded city

Two young sisters have come to relax and sit in their favorite play area. The older sister is untying a ribbon from a stuffed rabbit so her younger sister can wear it around her hair.

*I think, if they are here, did the mother leave them to beg from tourist?*

Entrance to a gated Cambodian shrine, a young girl begs for food.

A young boy sits pondering his deck of playing cards, while his friend sleeps a few feet away.

On a side note, many of the homeless boys reflect an international ambiance. With designer names and logo on their shirts and jeans. I think, *where would they get the money to purchase them, while denying themselves food and water?*

A young girl rests her head on the curb sleeping peacefully with a clown face sheet covering her body.

Thousands sleep on the streets and a boy smiles

Thousands of children, sleep wherever they want, and without a permanent address, show little regard for the dangers on the streets. They sleep on the sidewalks, even though some are robbed or worse, kidnapped. Given the downside of street life, and the possibility of prostitution, rape or death, the children still accept this life.

Crossing a busy street between tuk tuks is a challenge for this boy navigating his homemade wheelchair through a congested intersection. The boys legs are turned and twisted underneath his lower body, yet he has the arm strength to keep ahead of the slower moving bikes.

As the boy comes closer, I am not sure what to do. I think, *should I step back on the curb and wait or take his picture?* Before making the decision he looks at me and with the boy comes closerout any reservations on what I should do, he gives me the thumbs up.

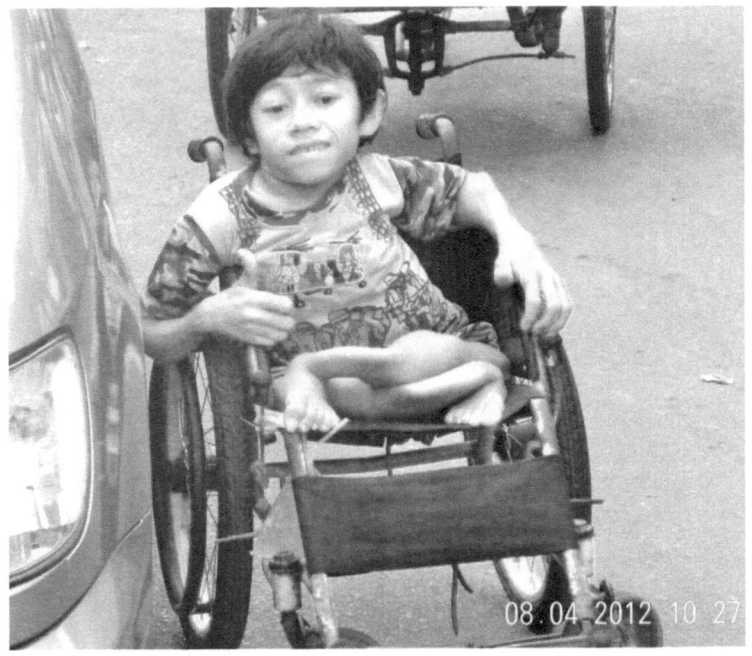

Young boy pushing through city traffic confined to his wheelchair. There are no government programs, or neighbors to help him.

No one walking nearby offers food or water

It's after five in the afternoon, and during a walk through the park, an elderly man sits blocking one of the crossing paths in a deliberate manner that people have to walk around him.

To his left is a large black trash bag that has everything he owns. His head is shaved, yet he looks clean, and his garment, though worn from years of use is unsoiled. From his viewpoint of many lonely years, he seems at peace with his long-suffering life, while tolerating those obvious glances.

A mother pulls the arm of her five-year old daughter, directing her around her right side, as they look away. No one walking nearby offers food, water, or money, yet he patiently sits watching both young and old continuing away from him. I too continue walking.

29.04.2012 17:25

An elderly man sits on the cross walk forcing others to walk around, yet hoping they will stop and give money or food.

Leaving the park a man standing in the gutter with his right hand out, talks to me in Khmer. I don't understand but I know he wants money. Offering a few Cambodian bills, totaling one U.S. dollar, he accepts them and smiles. I jester to take his picture. He shakes his head no, and motions for me to give him more money. I shake my head no, and that's when he walks away. I turn away and continue back to the hotel, but looking over my shoulder, I see him up against the temple wall … urinating. I take his picture for free.

Across from the Royal Palace
Park a homeless man urinates
against the temple wall.

A happy family and man who scares me

Five blocks from the hotel, a wooden fence towers on my left blocking entry into a construction site, yet there are no workers or construction equipment in the area.

It is good to see the city developing areas for housing, but since my arrival, I've noticed too many building sites started, and left unfinished. I'm not sure if it is a lack of investment capital by the government or corporations, or the lack of skilled workers, but the construction sit unattended. At this site the weeds grow through the fence, and any scrap and valuable items have been removed.

It is such properties that the street people [families] find, and make their home. The buildings aren't guarded by security so mom and dad with the children occupy the first floors. The hazards of unfinished floors, and the possibility of personal injury to the kids does not stop them from living there or the kids from playing.

Turning at the end of this fence, and between it and the building are piles of bricks, concrete and broken bamboo supports scattered about, clearly a hazard. However, a family is occupying the inside of the first floor as the children play among the broken glass and wood. Outside the main entrance, clothes hang on a rope, to dry while mom is inside fixing a meager meal for her children.

A family lives among the rubble and out of the rain providing some protection against roving teenage gangs

In a wheelchair and a dog to his right, a man in his mid-forties stares at me with cutting brown eyes, suggesting that I should not take his picture. His legs and feet are deformed, and possibly are the results from the Vietnam, Cambodian War when he was a child. His expression tells a sad story as a child who saw and felt too much pain, yet remembers images from a time of torture and murder. He was fortunate to have escaped then, but today his disability only reminds him of that past.

Man in a wheelchair with deformed legs. See chapters 4 and 5, reference to children stories from the Killing Fields and the S21 prison.

An old women wants to be noticed

Across from the park and the numerous bistros, indoor restaurants, and hotels overlook the Tonles Sap River. From these venues, hundreds of visiting tourist and locals visit this area to relax and savor the multi-national cuisines. This section is a favorite watering hole for those who enjoy time away from the cluttered housing and the chaotic traffic of Penh.

Part of the Sothearos Boulevard landscape is an elderly woman who sits outside a three-star restaurant. Her presence today is no different from any other previous day, and is a recognizable feature the owners allow. Camping against their restaurant wall [her favorite hangout] she is part of the colorful green and yellow shrubs behind her, a pleasant contrast to her unkempt hair, faded skirt, and pale colored blouse. Her clothes worn from sitting in the sun, and with an occasional bottle of water, comes here every day and endures her solitude hardship with an outstretched arm. Passer-bys may or may not drop a dollar into her white pot, yet she quietly maintains the calmness of spirit to continue.

Sandals to her side and with legs folded under her dress, an old woman sits on the sidewalk, begging with her timeworn white pot.

Many cannot march to a different drum

During the walks, I have seen an older generation of women and men with deformities, and thought, *do they receive any government assistance, or individual care from private organizations?* With the lack of proper nourishment, children contract polio, rickets, and other human deformities, and grow up with these impairments. They struggled as teens only to become old and worn, carrying their deformities, not as banners to evoke pity, but dragging them as symbols from an uncaring government. They may not have accepted it fully, but on a different level of humbleness, they are at ease with it.

Worse off than most, a man sits on the sidewalk. He is well dressed wearing plaid shorts and a white short-sleeve sport shirt, and flip-flops. He sells bags of dried fruit and children's trinkets for the Cambodian New Year, *Year of the Dragon.*

A legless man wears flip-flops on his hands to walk around the neighborhood.

There are more crippled children and adults in the cities of Phnom Penh and Siem Reap than any American city. Unlike the children in the United States who are hospitalized by caring organizations, the deformed child of Cambodia may receive some medical attention.

Due to a <u>severe</u> lack of qualified proffessionals the Cambodian medical services fails to meet international standards.

# CHAPTER 11
## The Light House Organization: Hope for the Homeless Child

Entrance to the Light House Organization (LHO), Au Andong Village, Sangkat Prek Pra, Khan Mean Chey, Phnom Penh, Cambodia. The wall donated by friends from Norway in 2008 is a grand entrance to a place of hope for the orphans from Phnom Penh.

After an early breakfast, my tuk tuk driver, Khunara, is driving to the Light House Organization Orphanage.

He says, "This place you can see orphans and its only 8 miles from the hotel."

"How long will it take to get there? I ask.

He says, "forty-three minutes."

The distance allows the necessary time to check notes and questions to ask the staff and children on arrival. I am curious as to how many children I will meet, and anxious to interview the staff who are (dedicated) to helping the orphans.

The Light House Organization is an institution operated by skilled professionals with the mission of caring for the children from the city and the farming areas around Phnom Penh, who would have been left on the streets, raped, or just die of hunger.

From their website, the following - Mission/Vision:

Vision: Education and love is the road to a better world. Together we help to enlighten children's futures. Our Mission: Light House provide is to empower underprivileged children and young through relevant education, innovative healthcare and care giving. Protecting children's right from any form of abuse and labor work.

Who they are: Lighthouse has been established since 2002, with the goal of providing a warm shelter to destitute unfortunate children living in harsh conditions. We started with very little material comfort but always with abundant of love and affection. Today the children enjoy improved living conditions thanks to the tireless effort of the director, volunteers, and our sponsors.

Mrs. Chea Savy, the director at the lighthouseorganizationlho@gmail.com

The way to help them is not always an easy path, yet it works

Driving through the country portrays a people living below the minimum poverty level, but they have two things in common - farming, and children. Children playing on the streets with whatever they can find or make from discarded lumber or sticks, like any child around the world would, and on their faces the same universal smile.

Smiles are the one quality most children have shown during the eleven-day stay thus far, but to say they are happy would be improper. In the United States, the pursuit of happiness deemed as our unalienable right, is a description that cannot apply for most of the children I have seen. They may not perceive happiness as we do, but a feeling of comfort and acceptance does suffice, because from their eyes they have seen sights few can imagine.

During our ride to the orphanage, Khunara ask. "Would you like to buy rice for the children?"

"That will be a good idea, but let me see how much it cost." I say, believing there is a choice of size and weights, "I want to wait before saying yes."

After twenty-minutes we arrive at a well-stocked shed a few minutes from the orphanage, and looking around the only rice they have cost $50.00 for a fifty-pound bag, and that is more than I can afford. "Khunara, I only have twenty-dollars, but I would like to buy something for the children."

Khunara adds, "why don't you buy them some sports equipment or writing tablets instead?"

"Now, that's a good idea," I say, "what would be the best ball for them?' Not knowing the area of the playing field, they have.

Khunara says, "a soccer ball would be the best choice."

Inside this mom and pop store are baseballs, basketballs, and soccer balls to one side of the hut. On the other side are colorful backpacks, stacks of writing tablets and enough pencils, and pens to choose from to make the children happy. After a few minutes, I decide to purchase a soccer ball and a dozen writing tablets and pencils to help the children, and within a few minutes, we are on our way.

A sign welcoming orphans to a place of hope

Khunara knows all too well the route to the orphanage, this is not the first time he's taken tourist to visit and see for themselves the good that's being accomplished. Khunara parks outside against the wall of the compound. The sign above tells the story of a meaningful organization about people who are doing their best with what they have for Phnom Penh's orphans.

The children's center contains living quarters and teaching buildings surrounded by a large wall insuring security for the children and staff. The large sign over the entrance invites visitors to enter and help where needed or to donate teaching aids, food, and sports equipment. I think, finally, a place where children don't beg for food.

At the pavilion, Khunara introduces me to the director and his staff sitting around picnic tables. I give the soccer ball and writing material to one of the assistance and I am thanked for my generosity. Khunara makes the initial introductions, and then goes to talk with his friends at one of the tables.

"Hello, my name is John."

A man approaches and says, "hello, I'm Jembe, a volunteer, and this is boss, Mr. Lee."

"Thank you," Mr. Lee says to the volunteer.

"Good afternoon," I say to Mr. Lee, "are you the manager of the school?"

"Yes." Mr. Lee says as he reaches out to shake my hand.

"Great. I'm writing a book about the children of Phnom Penh, and Khunara told me about this place and the children."

Mr. Lee is a robust man at five-foot seven with short hair, wearing fatigue pants and a pullover. I ask, shaking his hand. "I wanted to include in my book the work you are doing here with the children."

"Thank you, and what is your name again?" He ask.

"I'm John, from America."

"What part of America?" He ask as we walk to the main building.

"Texas. Do you know where Texas is?'

"Yes, I've heard of it."

I explain where New York City and California are, and at the ocean where Galveston, Texas is, and that is where I live.

Mr. Lee shakes his head that he knows Texas.

In the center area of the compound there is room to play ball, ride bikes, and a playground for the younger children.

I think, why there aren't any children in the grassy area or riding bikes. They may be eating lunch, but I would expect to see a few playing.

"Mr. Lee, where are the children?"

"They have been given a week off due to the country observing the Cambodian New Year, The Year of the Dragon. Mostly everyone in the city, including the children, went to the rural areas to stay with their families."

"Oh," I said with some disappointment. "I wanted to take a few photos while I was here of the children playing and studying."

"Sorry, John, the children," Mr. Lee tells me, "were put on buses, and transported to their homes a few days ago."

Regrouping my thoughts, I ask Mr. Lee. "I must say this is a larger area than I imagined, and I guess my next question is, what do the children learn?"

"We teach English, Khmer, and Cambodian to all the children, but mostly we want them to know English. However, it helps them to know more than one language."

As we continue walking toward one of the buildings, I ask Mr. Lee. "With all the children you teach, where do they come from?"

"Mostly from the rural areas, but some do come from the city." Mr. Lee says with a smile of accomplishment.

"How many children do you have here at one time?"

"We began in 2003 with fifteen children, and now we have one-hundred and eight."

"Wow, that's a lot of mouths to feed. What do you feed them?"

"We feed rice mostly," he says.

I ask, "do they eat anything else?" Thinking that can't be all they eat.

Mr. Lee tells me. "Yes, they have vegetables and meat sometimes when we can get it."

"How much rice does it take to feed all the children?" I ask.

"Twenty-five kilograms last one week and that amount also include ten staff members.

I ask, "do you receive any donations to feed them, and to buy school supplies?"

He looked at his volunteers. "During the months of January through March we have many volunteers come here to help, and then when they leave they send money and supplies."

"Other than the rice and vegetables, how do you and your staff care for the children?"

"We receive medicine from outside organizations [mostly] from Asia."

"Does your organization receive any government support?"

"No, just other organizations outside the country send us money, and a few like ourselves, who can afford it," he says.

He was positive on the help sent him, but I gather he was always struggling to find other means to support these children.

"How do others know of the work you are doing here?" I ask.

"Well, it is from the volunteer's word of mouth returning to their own country."

"Do the volunteers come to help the kids, or send money?" I ask.

"We get a lot of visitors that come in January, February, and March, and then when they return home send what they can afford," he says.

I ask. "Where do the majority of people come from?" I paused to catch up, he has a brisk walk. "What countries?"

"A lot from the neighboring countries and of course Europe and America, but generally from Singapore," he says, "a lot of volunteers come from outside the country to help, but it is the people from China who spend more time with the children."

In some buildings where the smaller children sleep two or three in a bed, the rooms have painted animals and flowers on the walls and the children have their own storage areas for school supplies under the beds. The older teenagers sleep in another building.

After talking for a few minutes about the support from his friends in China, Mr. Lee and I exchanged email addresses. Passing an open pavilion, I take two group photos of his staff before touring the other buildings. I think, the books, pencils, and pens would be put to good use, and of course the soccer ball. I ask, "what happens to the older teenagers who require additional education?"

"Those who are seventeen we send them to city schools for more advanced classes."

I ask. "Where are they today?"

"They are with their extended families for the New Year celebration."

Inside one of the buildings, the sleeping area for the children is close together, but I know with that many children they can't have their own bed. "Are all the buildings empty?" I ask.

"Yes, they are, because of the holiday," he says, "but when they are here we look out for all of the children because the families are poor. They may have a mother and father but they are too poor to take care of them." Mr. Lee pauses, looking at his cell phone, he continues. "Some families cannot take care of their own children, so they send them to live here for us to feed and educate."

"When they go for the holiday do their parents pick them up or do you send them to a central point?" I ask.

"We send them by bus to their home town, and the family members there pick them up. After the holiday we send the bus back to pick all the children up and bring them back here to the school," he says.

The buildings look well kept, colorful, and not run down, plus the sanitary conditions of the dorms and the outside are clean and in good condition. There is a large play area in the middle of the compound, big enough for them to ride their bikes and play soccer.

"Do you have help with all these children? Like anyone from UNICEF or other worldwide organizations?" I ask.

"We have volunteers who are certified to teach and care for the children, but they do not come from the UK or UNICEF. They came here at their own expense and wanted to teach. We have many who teach English."

I ask, "how long do they stay?"

He says, "they usually spend a couple of days or a week here before returning home. A couple teachers have stayed here for a month, I am very grateful to them."

"Mr. Lee, do you have any other offices in Phnom Penh?"

"No, this is the only place where we care for the orphans."

I ask, "do you and all the staff members live here?"

"I and most of the staff do, but we have a few who live close by who come here four or five times a week to help."

After a tour around the grounds and the students sleeping quarters, I follow Mr. Lee into the main dining area. Between the staff's quarters, and one of the children's huts, is a large, open two-sided building on the edge of the playground with a closed room at the rear, where the bicycles and soccer balls are locked up.

"Here is the main dining room where we feed the children. It isn't large enough to feed all the children at one time so we have different times for each age group."

The area inside the building has open areas to the front facing the courtyard at one end, while the other end of the building is a storage room. I think, they may have a logistical problem feeding so many.

"Mr. Lee, how do you feed all the children their meals in such a small area?"

"Let me show you, John." He walks back and forth and shows me where in the middle they place the tables in such a manner that most of the children can eat inside together.

"Mr. Lee, it's obvious not all the children can eat at one time."

"That's right, some eat on the outside, but this is the main area. A majority of the children are young and small so it might be a squeeze for some, but I believe they have fun sitting close together."

I say, "there's a few tables and chairs, so do the children sit on the grass?"

"We don't have many tables, but the picnic tables on the outside we bring in when we serve the meals."

"Looks like you have more tables than bikes."

"The bikes," he says laughingly, "are for exercising, so we have more bikes for the children to ride than chairs to sit and eat."

"Makes sense to me." I say, laughing with him.

I ask, "what happens, Mr. Lee if the children get sick, or hurt themselves during the day?"

He tells me, "we can treat minor cuts and bruises, and have a dispensary with some medicines."

"Do you have a doctor on call for the more serious aches and pains?"

"Yes, we have a doctor we call during the day or night, and then we pay him later. He lives close."

"What happens if a child breaks an arm or a leg?"

Mr. Lee says, "we take them to the children's hospital in Phnom Penh."

"Do you have doctors from other countries that come here to help?" I ask.

"Yes, we have volunteers that come from the outside, from other Asian countries, but they are usually dentist." Mr. Lee stops for a moment to look at his cell phone again. "Doctors don't usually come here often. In 2005, two foreign doctors and dentist came for a few days to treat the children, and gave medicine. We were very thankful for them."

There are two dorms set aside for teaching the children, and following Mr. Lee into one building, I notice how colorful the outside looks. Brightly painted with blues and yellows, and animals painted near the entrance for a happier approach to learning.

One child sits at the computer console typing while two friends watch, as well as Mr. Lee. On the front wall are three signs. One sign is about insects, another one on the English letters with examples, and one that strikes me more than the world map to their left ... a sign above that reads; all students must speak English during the class.

I ask Mr. Lee, standing next to the computer. "Who teaches the children? Is it you or one of the staff members?"

"We had two qualified teachers from Norway who volunteered their services a few months ago, and I asked them to stay, they said yes, and have been with us for many months."

"How much time do the children spend in classes and what do they learn?' At this point Mr. Lee received another call on his cell phone and motions that I should watch the students on the computer.

As I watch them navigate through the English language, and how easy they are using the Internet, I look around the classroom. The room has many desks on both sides, similar to America's old prairie schoolhouses, and yet they serve the purpose. Mr. Lee is done talking, and smiles, walking back into the room.

"Do the children have enough time for playing, and how long is a typical day in school for them?" I think, they may spend too much time studying, especially learning three languages.

Mr. Lee says, "the children spend time on the playground, but they don't have much free time during the week. They must spend time learning English and Khmer. They spend two hours a day learning English, one hour Khmer, and are in class for six hours every day."

"How much time do they spend outside the class playing on the field?" I ask.

Mr. Lee says. "Recreation is part of their program, and we have them play soccer ball, or just exercising, but our main concern is their schooling. On the weekends they play soccer and ride bikes."

"Do you have many older teenagers, and what happens when they get too old to live here, like you said earlier about them reaching seventeen?"

"Sorry."

Mr. Lee was getting an email on his phone and turned away out of the sun to read it. After a few minutes, Mr. Lee returns with a smile on his face. "Mr. Lee what happens when they reach seventeen years of age?"

"We have a policy. At the age of seventeen-years old, and if someone on the outside wants to sponsor them they can stay, but when they are eighteen they must leave to find work or more education in another school or university in Phnom Penh. If they aren't smart enough we send them to the NGO for trade education."

NGO encompasses local and worldwide organizations to promote activities and additional education for children in countries around the globe. A few are, The American Red Cross, The Cambodian Women's Crisis Center, Mith Samlanh Friends, The Cambodian Trust, and others from Japan and China as well.

In the center of an open field of grass and dirt a play area has a new climbing fixture with a seesaw, swings, and nearby a small basketball court. The center is large enough for children to play soccer and ride bikes.

Entrance to one of the children's buildings is a painted blue elephant on the left side of the entrance, and a pink one is on the opposite side. The older children painted the animals.

## A good day at the orphanage

Mr. Lee said earlier that the older boys stay with the younger boys, because there are more boys than girl orphans, their dorms are larger. The girl's dorms are "girlish" [author's note] with colorful brightly painted animals on the walls, of bright blue, red, and yellow, and even the bed linen have colorful animal designs.

Mr. Lee places a lot of emphasis on studying to prepare the children with a first-class education, paying (particular) attention to the language and math skills, specifically with English and Khmer. The policy is sound, because at eighteen if they don't have a proper education they will place them in a trade school, to continue their training.

I'd like to stay longer, because while I did not see or talk to the children, the experience and knowledge gained from this group of concerned people gives me hope for a few of the orphans of Phnom Penh. I glance at Khunara, my driver, and see he is anxious to leave. He nods, meaning he would like to leave and prepare for the Cambodian New Year. He mentioned earlier that he wanted to stop for a bag of mangos for his wife and be with his children. I smile and shake my head yes, he smiles.

I bow and say a Khmer good-bye, and then shaking hands with Mr. Lee, motion for all to sit around the picnic table for one final picture. It is a hot day and the staff is sitting underneath the pavilion roof, resting, and drinking water. They all smile and wave as Khunara and I walk through the gate for home. I know Mr. Lee was happy with my visit.

Talking with Khunara on the way back he thanked me for visiting this place, because when I asked him yesterday if he knew how to get here, he immediately said yes. He had taken others here, and he has two boys and a girl and was grateful he could feed them, and what I just did made him happy that I care what happens to the children in a another country, it is a good day.

A mile down the road we stop to buy a large quantity of mangos for Khunara's family. I had noticed during the preceding four days many street vendors selling assorted fruits and colorful flowers. It is a tradition in Cambodia to bring in the New Year with fresh items, such as fruit or colorful flowers.

Khunara tells me. "Bananas are very common for the celebration and a great tribute to the New Year, but they don't taste as sweet as mangos, and my children like the taste."

The Cambodian people look forward to the start of the most colorful time of the year, the beginning of this year - The Year of The Dragon.

They purchase fresh fruit and colorful flowers to welcome in the new year 2556, with a three-day celebration, April 13, 14, and 15 of the month that concludes the Buddhist year of 2555.

The population is thankful and delighted to show their family and friends the grace toward, the new-year angel, Kemira Tevy. She wears a hairpin of violet flowers, carries a sword in her right hand, and a zither in her left. The sixth daughter of Kabil Moha Prum rides a water buffalo, and all give her a special offering of bananas. The entire house decorated with fresh flowers invites her to come in and bless them and their home.

The Light House Organization, and seeing the good they do, is a welcome respite from the despair of the children living in poverty. Two weeks since arriving was spent photographing the unpleasant side of the city, so this break from that heartbreaking journey is appreciated.

On the return trip over a bridge leading into Phnom Penh, and near the water's edge are huts that make up the "Water's-Edge Slums," a depressed community, housing one of the poorest of the city. In the background is a high-rise apartment complex on the left, and a modern hotel to the right. The vivid contrast between the progress and the slums is evident throughout the city, and not only confined to this area, but this shantytown was a cultural shock.

# CHAPTER 12
## I Saw the Absurdity of Phnom Penh

During the last four-weeks, I became (vividly) aware of the depth of the people's suffering and of the silent cries for help from the *Street Children*. The knowledge from my observations provided an insight unlike any reading material I could have discovered prior to leaving Texas. I appreciated the first hand accounts that provided a unique opportunity in understanding the dramatic differences this society endures and yet condones. I also became aware of the resilient attitude of these same struggling people, and weighing the good and not so pleasant lives they face every day, a lesson in humility.

The mindset of America's homeless to support themselves comes from a street culture's survival code, <u>not to depend on others</u>. They derive this training from years of living in areas of the city that have restaurants and places to sleep, and with dumpsters that provide, along with <u>soup kitchens</u>, a minimal degree of sustained existence when necessary.

Within a country that does little to use their unlimited resources of food, water, and finances, and the government and corporate agendas unwilling to stay the long-term course, it is no wonder the majority of America lives with an apathetic perception of right and wrong for the homeless.

America's affluent society tends to balance itself on the easiest ways to care for the homeless, against having the homeless fend for themselves, knowing that America cares little for them. Like Cambodia, the American homeless are defensive of what is theirs and leery of a government they distrust.

Lacking education, Phnom Penh children not able to mentally embrace or understand the cities changing times settle for the way it has always been. Their effort for repetition as a way of life for their survival is as correct to them as it is illogical to me. They endure this street life by instinct, and not by choice, and for the hundreds who don't know an easier way, and without the cities support many will die.

Cambodia is many countries, Phnom Penh is many cities

This report is not a comparison of the United States to Cambodia, for I expected the change in climate, cultures, and the people. It is however, about Phnom Penh, and what the children see.

What is it about a child's eyes; calming, pleading, happy for the smallest amount of attention that allows one to wonder about this city's future? It is the absurdity of the Phnom Penh government and the contradictions and inconsistencies they created. Unfortunately, my western thinking was measuring their political views by the standards *I believe* they should apply.

Americans have choices, or at the very least offerings they can accept or ignore, but not so in Phnom Penh. Take a national sampling of those freedoms in America, transplant them to Cambodia, and then condense them into a city of 2 million people, and anything good of a caring American idea, will die.

The reason they fail is that Mr. Hun Sen's repressive rule is a "soft dictatorship". He is misusing the lawful rights of the people, specifically, the working middle class and the poor, for the sake of tourism.

Sen's political warfare on the Cambodian people pits his wealthy upper class backers against eighty percent of those who work to survive.

His ideology, liken to Pol Pot, will not falter, because countries outside of Cambodia fail to apply financial and political pressure on his agenda.

Modern high rises,the Phnom Penh Tower and the Gold Tower at Monivong and Sihanouk Blvd. are three blocks away, where children live in concrete pipes.

# CHAPTER 13
## Revolutionary Phnom Penh;
## Chaos on the Capitol Streets


February 2014, news reports published on Phnom Penh revealed Cambodia's thinking toward its own citizens. The first week of January, government military police shot and <u>killed</u> five garment workers during their <u>peaceful protest</u> for a higher minimum wage. On the Vent Sleng Boulevard, many other striking workers, during the peaceful rally were injured and severely beaten. The garment workers are presently making $100.00 a month and wanted $160.00 a month.

Feeling the "iron-hand" rule of *Prime Minister Sen's Cambodia People's Party,* over twenty demonstrators were detained without due process of law during their passive rally against the corrupt national election of 2013, felt the "iron-hand" rule of Prime Minister Hun Sen's Cambodia People's Party. A bloody coup by Hun Sen against his opposition took into custody those detainees. Many were arrested, tortured, and exiled, and unknown number were *immediately executed* for their right to oppose Sen. During an opposition rally in 1997, led by Sam Rainsy, grenades killed sixteen people and injured more than 100, some who died later from their wounds. The actions of the Killing fields and recent murders differ on the numbers and how death is dealt, but the history of Cambodia will not.

Since 1991, the Paris Peace Agreements, intended to secure the peace and democracy of every citizen in Cambodia, has not held with the current government's policy. Not since the demise of the Khmer Rouge's rule, has the government faced civil unrest in such a monumental scale, and by their action, China and other supporting countries are limiting their much needed financial aid.

In November 2014, a government decision to raise the <u>monthly minimum</u> wage in the garment industry to $128.00, outraged labor unions stating it is too little, while employers claimed such a large raise could close factories.

> Three things cannot be long hidden: the sun, the
> moon, and the truth.
>
> Buddha

# CHAPTER 14
## From the Eyes of Children, Horror and Hope

Do not forget me sir. I have little hope and for today.
You don't know my sorrow. You can't feel my pain.
Tell someone to care.

~~~

Today my mommy tells me to walk the street. I do my best.
Don't yell at me mom. I am only four.

~~~

After leaving a city school the younger boy is pushed by his older brother.
They are collecting recyclable items to take back to their parents.

~~~

I pray to the winds, the sun for I want to sleep, to
escape. Buddha, take me quick, I am tired.

~~~

*Better than a thousand hollow words, is one word that brings peace.*
Buddha

~~~

Somedays I accept my life. Everyday I know this hell,
It is mine alone. Someone steady this chair.
It has replaced my legs.

~~~

This young boy may not have a permanent home, or living relatives, or
eaten today, but he hopes someone will remember him. The eyes tell a story
of how he lives on the streets, quiet and alone.

~~~

If it rains today, I will be clean. I am dirty and I smell.
Is that why you look away?

~ ~ ~


~ ~ ~

Speak for us stranger. Let them know what you saw.
After you go, we stay. Tell all about this agony,
this torment. Tell someone we still live.

~ ~ ~


~ ~ ~

These formidable guardians inside a Buddha's compound have watched over Cambodia and guarded the monks for centuries. Through the Vietnam/Cambodia War, they remain custodians of the past.

Leaders of the Cambodian people.

# Epilogue

The people of Phnom Penh are stern and quiet but because of the language barrier, I could not get a better depiction of their lives. I believe though, the message of the Cambodian citizen is not to be denied, as are those thousands of children living on the streets.

After thirty-days in Phnom Penh, my opinions of the city and its people are dramatically changed. The assumptions prior to landing at the airport was of a crowded city, stacked houses, numerous hotels, and Asian restaurants. Today, with a better understanding of **how** they live, no matter their place in society, I leave thinking, I know how, but not why they continue. The poor are not physically strong, yet their nature somehow pushes them to another day. How do they do it? I say out loud, "I don't know."

Revealing the story of children living on the streets as literate, dirty and want is correct. They live on the filth of sidewalks, in abandon buildings, smell from urine, yet from their eyes see more of the city than the elders, they see the pointlessness.

Could more be said with another story or photograph of a failed government project or showing one more suffering child? Maybe, but when would my obligation to 24,000 children end?

Are the conclusions of the Phnom Penh government as they deal with the public accurate? Yes, yet behind closed doors they are hiding their true policy from the people. [Ed]

Eating in a local Chinese restaurant, a conversation with a couple from China ends with this.

Sir, I ask, "do you and your wife come to Phnom Penh often?"

He finishes his tea and says, "my wife and I come here once a year, to enjoy the beauty of the city."

I ask, "have you noticed the children begging at the restaurants?"

He pauses, "we see little boys and girls walking around," looking across the table he tells me, "we give money sometimes, but there aren't that many, so we feel good."

I'm not sure what he means, so I say good-bye and leave. I think, *he doesn't have a clue what's going on in this city.*

> "A man asked Gautama Buddha, "I want happiness."
> Buddha said, "First remove "I," that's Ego, then remove "want," that's Desire. See now you are left with only "Happiness."
>
> — Gautama Buddha, Sayings Of Buddha

==========================